S0-DTC-221

The Legacy of Che Guevara

The Legacy of Che Guevara

A Documentary Study

DONALD C. HODGES

THAMES AND HUDSON

Documents translated by
Ernest C. Rehder and Donald C. Hodges

Any copy of this book issued by the publisher
as a paperback is sold subject to the condition
that it shall not, by way of trade or otherwise,
be lent, re-sold, hired out, or otherwise
circulated without the publisher's prior consent,
in any form of binding or cover other than that in
which it is published and without a similar
condition including this condition being imposed
on a subsequent purchaser.

© 1977 THAMES AND HUDSON LTD, LONDON

All rights reserved. No part of this publication
may be reproduced or transmitted in any form or
by any means, electronic or mechanical, including
photocopy, recording or any information
storage and retrieval system, without permission
in writing from the publisher.

Filmset and printed in Great Britain by
BAS Printers Limited, Wallop, Hampshire

Contents

Introduction

Italicized numerals in brackets refer to the Documents

The New Left in Latin America is virtually indistinguishable from the political currents generated by the Cuban Revolution in response to the common Latin American predicament of underdevelopment. The social basis of revolutionary movements in Latin America may be traced to a number of broad factors. A frustrated sense of patriotism is the response to the dominating role of foreign, mainly US-based, corporations which appear to manipulate Latin American governments in their own interest and have the effect of distorting the independent development of native economies. The symbols of prosperity in foreign business communities contrast starkly with the very low wages and squalid living conditions of native employees, while Latin American governments find themselves financially and technologically dependent on the US for the development of their national industries. On the analogy of the first War of Independence against Spanish colonialism (1810–25), Latin American revolutionaries conceive of the present struggle against US imperialism as a Second War of Independence. In Latin America power lies with a landed oligarchy, native capitalists linked to foreign interests, and the armed forces which often have imposed unpopular governments on their countries in violation of electoral results. Corrupt electoral practices, governments which give only lip service to their constitutions, and military dictatorships which arbitrarily establish their own grounds of legitimacy – all these form the background against which the New Left has been active.

If revolutionary violence has become an accepted political tactic in Latin America, its origins should be related to the institutionalization of violence by Latin American governments, which attribute their difficulties to popular discontent and to communist subversion rather than to their own failures. Largely impotent to solve their countries' fundamental social and economic problems, they have turned to the US for aid, thereby accentuating their dependence. They have mistaken symptoms for causes and in many cases escalated repression against their own people. The origins of guerrilla warfare on the continent, therefore, are to be traced not only to the political currents unloosed by the Cuban Revolution, but to an institutionalized tradition of violence to which the Cuban Revolution itself was a response.

Historically, Guevarism represents the culmination or convergence of popular responses to this violence. Its foundations were laid in 1960 with the publication of Che's manual on *Guerrilla Warfare*. Selected as early as 1959 to supervise the allocation of Cuban manpower, money and munitions to those insurrectional centers struggling against other military dictatorships, Che took charge of internationalizing the Cuban Revolution and of converting the Cordillera of the Andes into the Sierra Maestra of Latin America.

Later, with the launching of Che's Bolivian campaign in April 1967 and the almost simultaneous publication of his 'Message to the Tricontinental', Guevarism emerged as a revolutionary tendency independent of the Cuban Revolution. By launching the Bolivian guerrillas, Che was to become identified by many as a new Bolívar at the head of an international army for the liberation of Latin America from the indirect economic and political tutelage of the United States. Although that army was financed and recruited with Cuban assistance, Che was in sole command. The effort to create a Latin American 'Vietnam' in Bolivia transformed Guevarism from a current within the Cuban Revolution into a closely related but distinct revolutionary tendency, whose differences with Castroism were to become conspicuous only after Che's death.

Since then, Che's followers have divided into sharply opposing political factions. Today Guevarism is represented by a composite of political movements and is far from constituting a coherent political trend. As a consequence, the partisans of Fidel Castro and many Guevarist movements no longer see eye to eye. In Peru, Fidel's followers are on the side of the military junta; most Guevarists are opposed to it. The Cuban government has mostly praise for the nationalist regime of Omar Torrijos in Panama, while Guevarist groups continue to resist the military dictatorship. And in Mexico, whose populist government has remained on friendly terms with Castro, Guevarist-inspired urban and rural guerrillas have proliferated without restraint.

Che's legacy contains an indiscriminate blending, overlapping and confusion of intellectual and practical contributions to different areas of behavior that should be separated and distinguished. First, there is Che the insurrectionary theorist, strategist and tactician. This is the main thrust of his legacy, and it weighs heavily on his post-1967 followers and on interpreters of the Latin American left. Second, there is Che the economic theorist and planner. This second body of material is predicated on the first, peripheral to it and thus far applicable only to the Cuban experience. Third, there is Che the guerrilla hero, the martyr and myth. This romantic and glamorous aspect of his legacy has captivated young people and misled them into believing that revolutions are made simply by taking up the gun. Experienced revolutionaries are not deceived by the heroic image of Che as the new man of the twentieth century; indeed, they have frankly discouraged this cult of personality as an expression of youthful but misdirected idealism. In Latin America, as elsewhere, it is apparent that seemingly unending and often dull tasks are necessary to the building of a revolutionary movement.

To present a picture of the foundations of Guevarism, its divisions, its impact on Third World liberation movements, and its newly discovered role in the advanced countries, is the object of this essay and of the documents that follow. Each major heading and subheading of the Introduction corresponds to a set of related texts presented in the same order. The issues debated in the documents may be clarified by turning to the relevant section of the Introduction, which places them in political perspective.

The development of Guevarism

An account of the evolution of Guevarism must, wherever possible, consider Che's own explanations of how and why this development took place. Although his politics and strategy evolved within a Marxist–Leninist framework, they did so within a specific social setting. Unlike Fidel, Che did not originally choose politics as his profession. He explained his growing interest in politics, in an August 1960 speech on revolutionary medicine, in terms of special circumstances that led him to give up a medical career for that of a professional revolutionary. Originally, he had hoped to excel in some branch of medical research. But having traveled throughout Latin America, he was struck by the misery, hunger and illness of the people and by the lack of adequate medical facilities. He soon became convinced that it was just as important to help these people directly as to make an original contribution to medical science. In Guatemala he began making notes on what would have to be done in order to practice medicine in a revolutionary way. These were interrupted by a military invasion of Guatemala financed by the United Fruit Company and the CIA, intent on stopping the agrarian reform launched by the radical government of Jacobo Arbenz. It was then, Che tells us, that he learned that to become a revolutionary doctor, one must first make a revolution.

Che's account of the impact of his Guatemalan experience appears in an April 1958 interview with the Argentine journalist, Jorge Masetti. In answer to the question whether he had a position in the democratic government of Jacobo Arbenz, Che replied: 'No, but when the North American [sponsored] invasion took place I tried to organize a group of young men like myself to fight the adventurers. In Guatemala . . . it was necessary to resist, but hardly anyone wanted to.' Again, in response to a question on why he joined the Cuban revolutionaries, Che replied: 'In reality, after the experience I went through . . . and the Guatemalan ending, not much was needed to convince me to join any revolution against a tyrant.' A year later, in answer to a similar question posed in an interview by Cuba's

Telemundo Televisión, he said: 'I saw how democracy was destroyed in Guatemala, and when I met Fidel in Mexico I considered it my duty to help him destroy the [Cuban] dictatorship.'

Unlike Fidel, who turned to Marxism–Leninism as late as December 1961, Che had already embraced it in Guatemala in June 1954. While Castroism emerged as a left-wing trend within Cuba's popular democratic party and did not approach communist positions until almost a decade later, Guevarism evolved from the first within a Marxist–Leninist framework. In *Ernesto: A Memoir of Che Guevara* (Garden City, N.Y., 1972), his first wife, Hilda Gadea, claims that Che had belonged for a short time to the Communist Youth in Argentina and was already well versed in revolutionary Marxism when he joined Fidel's July 26 Movement in Mexico – a movement launched by Cuban exiles for the purpose of overthrowing the dictatorship in their country. She also recalls how in Guatemala Che talked openly about his communist convictions and how, on arriving in Mexico City in October 1954, he affirmed that communists should be in the vanguard of every armed struggle against Latin American dictators.

The lessons of the frustrated agrarian and social reforms in Guatemala constituted the subject of Che's first political essay, 'I witnessed the fall of Jacobo Arbenz', written in the summer of 1954 during the invasion. According to Hilda Gadea's reconstruction of the essay from memory, it began with an analysis of the world situation and the struggle between the capitalist and socialist camps. Che anticipated that the socialist camp would continue to expand and that, in view of the overall struggle against imperialism, major efforts toward social change required a confrontation with US economic interests. With evident sympathy for the Chinese side in the Sino–Soviet conflict, he held that policies designed to promote the peaceful co-existence of socialism and capitalism constituted a betrayal of the national liberation struggles in Asia, Africa and Latin America. Only through the nationalization of basic resources and the socialization of the means of production, Che insisted, could the struggle for independent social development succeed. Furthermore, he argued that the confrontation with the native oligarchies and with the main enemy, US imperialism, had to be an armed one supported by the people. He believed that, if Arbenz had only armed the people, his government might have survived.

Later, in his reflections on the Cuban Revolution, Che underscored the need to educate the people in armed self-defense. The Guevarist insurrectional foco or center is a revolutionary commune for living and fighting together. Its principal task is to catalyze the masses into taking independent action in defense of what are taken to be their basic interests. Since people have reason to fear repression and are generally unprepared to resist a military coup against a popular government, they have to be educated for that eventuality from the start. Moreover, they have to be encouraged by the exploits of the insurrectional foco to follow its example and to provide armed support for a popular movement of resistance.

At the same time, the revolutionary vanguard must also be educated. Although the foco's first responsibility is to train revolutionary fighters, it is also dedicated to molding the new or communist man. A persistent revolutionary struggle against highly unfavorable odds requires morale as well as military skills. Since this morale depends on the cultivation of qualities of character not ordinarily achieved in bourgeois society, the insurrectional foco is also a school for creating the new man. For guerrillas compelled to associate with one another under conditions of maximum physical and psychological stress, the development of self-discipline was a virtual necessity.

The education of the new man is a matter of will as well as intelligence. While acknowledging that a correct assessment of historical conditions is a *sine qua non* of a viable revolutionary movement, Che also stressed the importance of human will in history. It was not necessary to wait for all the conditions of revolution to be given; the insurrectional foco could create them. The importance of human will is no less evident in Che's summary of the principal tasks of the postinsurrectionary phase. Not all the conditions for socialism have to be present before it becomes feasible; the vanguard party can create them. Whether the vanguard consists ·

of guerrilla fighters or party cadres, the model man forces the march of events to the limits of the objectively possible – that is the substance of Che's revolutionary strategy.

IMPACT OF THE CUBAN REVOLUTION

The most important factor in the shaping of Che's politics and strategy of revolution was the Cuban guerrilla experience. Each major stage in the development of the guerrilla forces led to a different assessment of Cuban social and political reality and a corresponding change in strategy. As Che records in 'Notes for the Study of the Ideology of the Cuban Revolution' (October 1960), prior to Castro's return from Mexico in December 1956 a subjectivist mentality prevailed: the unreasoned confidence in a popular upheaval which, combined with spontaneous revolutionary strikes by organized labor, would topple the dictatorship in short order (2). After Castro's initial landing on the *Granma* and the almost total destruction of the rebel forces, the guerrillas realized that the struggle would be a long one, that it was unrealistic to count on a spontaneous mass uprising, and that the peasants would have to be incorporated into the struggle. Accordingly, the guerrillas turned their attention from the administrative corruption and dishonesty of the ruling clique – the concern of the Cuban Orthodox Party to which Fidel had belonged – to the problems encountered by the peasants and their lack of land. They hoped to win the support of the peasants by offering them an agrarian reform.

With the March 1958 assassination of Frank País, a leader of the July 26 Movement in Santiago de Cuba, the people of that city took to the streets in protest. There followed the first political general strike against the dictatorship which, despite its lack of political direction, completely paralyzed the province of Oriente with repercussions on the neighboring province of Camagüey. This spontaneous mass uprising was easily crushed. But, as Che recalls in his 'Social Projections of the Rebel Army' (January 1959), it made the guerrillas aware for the first time of the need to incorporate the working class, and not only the peasantry, in the overall struggle for liberation. Thus began the first clandestine efforts to organize the workers in their centers of production for the purpose of helping the Rebel Army in its struggle to seize power. At the same time, this strategy was used by the civilian leaders of the July 26 Movement to relegate the armed struggle to the status of an engine or catalyst of a mass general strike under predominantly civilian leadership. It was only after the disastrous general strike, called without sufficient preparation for 9 April 1958, that another qualitative change occurred within the revolutionary movement, perhaps the most important for the final outcome of the insurrectionary struggle. That was the conviction that a victory over the Cuban dictator Batista could be achieved only through the continuous growth of the guerrilla forces, to which the political general strike would have to be auxiliary.

It would be a mistake to assume, however, that Che's own political development during this period corresponded in every case to his account of the political changes undergone by the bulk of the guerrilla forces. As early as November 1957, for example, he wrote an editorial for the mimeographed organ of the Rebel Army, *El Cubano Libre*, in which the political general strike was singled out as the decisive weapon in the revolutionary arsenal (1). As a Marxist–Leninist, he attached far more importance to the role of organized labor in the revolution than did the guerrillas who had come out of the Cuban Orthodox Party, who were mainly interested in restoring the constitution and calling new elections. Moreover, in 'One Year of Combat', also published in *El Cubano Libre* (January 1958), he concluded with a commitment to carry the revolution forward beyond a mere victory over Batista, so that it would be impossible ever to return to the old mode of governing – a conviction shared by only a small handful of the Rebel Army.

The Cuban experience contributed to Che's transformation from a people's physician not only into a guerrilla fighter and commander, but also into the economic tsar of the Cuban economy. Beginning as

President of the National Bank, Che was promoted to Minister of Industries in charge of industrialization. In 'Notes for the Study of the Ideology of the Cuban Revolution', Che himself stressed the differences between the insurrectionary and postinsurrectionary stages of the Cuban Revolution: the first stage of armed action lasting to 1 January 1959; and, after that, the second stage of political, economic and social transformation (2).

During the postinsurrectionary phase, however, Che continued to be concerned with problems of armed strategy, and in 1965 he renounced his role as supreme director of Cuban industry to return to that of a guerrilla commander. Among his reasons for doing so was the conviction that the parallel construction of socialism and communism in Cuba depended for its success on opening new revolutionary fronts in the Third World and in Latin America in particular. The development of Che's thought was accordingly more complex than his own two-stage analysis of the Cuban Revolution might suggest. In fact, his theory of the origins of revolution and his discussion of the problems involved in trying to start one belong to the period after 1 January 1959, when the postinsurrectionary phase of the Revolution provided a base for launching armed struggles throughout the rest of Latin America.

A study of the development of Che's thought should help correct the mistake of identifying his developed strategy of the insurrectional foco with the strategy he in fact applied during the insurrectionary phase of the Revolution. As we have seen, his strategy of armed struggle originally relied on the political general strike to overthrow the Batista dictatorship; only after the frustrated general strike of April 1958 did he begin to stress primarily a military confrontation with Batista. Yet the importance of such a strike should not be underestimated. The general strike called during the first days of January 1959 paralyzed the economy and permitted the Rebel Army to seize power directly, without a negotiated settlement with representatives of the regular army.

Only with the closing of the insurrectionary phase did Che begin to reflect seriously upon the theoretical problems posed by the Cuban

Revolution. One such problem was whether the Revolution constituted a counter-example to Lenin's thesis that 'without a revolutionary theory there can be no revolutionary movement'. Che's 'Notes for the Study of the Ideology of the Cuban Revolution' indicate that the Cuban insurrection was successful without its leaders having had more than a superficial acquaintance with Marxism–Leninism and its general laws of capitalist development (2). In Cuba, practice seems to have preceded a theory of the social conditions required to make a revolution.

Another problem was how to interpret the meaning of revolutionary theory. In order to launch a revolution and lead the masses to victory, one had to have a theory based on present realities and not merely a series of lessons culled from past revolutionary struggles. What is crucial to revolutionary theory in the practical context of making a revolution, Che argued, is a correct interpretation of concrete historical conditions and a correct assessment of the present balance of social forces. In short, a revolutionary theory has to be continually recreated and adapted to each new revolutionary situation.

This in turn requires a knowledge of the objective conditions which must be present in order for a revolutionary struggle to succeed – conditions first outlined by Che in 'Cuba: Historical Exception or Vanguard of the Anticolonial Struggle?' (April 1961). In that essay the objective origin of revolutions is traced to a condition euphemistically known as 'underdevelopment' (3). Those countries are underdeveloped whose development has been distorted through the cultivation for export of a few primary products under the domination of a landowning class in league with foreign interests. For the masses, the common denominator of underdevelopment consists of low wages, underemployment and unemployment. Che calls this condition the 'hunger of the people'. The objective conditions of revolution include this hunger of the people, the popular discontent generated by that hunger, the repression of the people, and the wave of hatred and resentment elicited by such repression. These conditions, Che believed, are present in virtually every Latin

American country. What are lacking are the subjective conditions of revolution, mainly the awareness that victory is possible only through the waging of armed struggle.

Unlike Lenin, for whom the objective conditions meant those necessary to seize power in the wake of a nation-wide political crisis, Che stressed the need to launch insurrections prior to such a crisis. The rationale for this departure from classic Leninism was that in Latin America the launching of an insurrection was necessary to prepare the subjective conditions of the struggle for power. In Latin America there was little prospect that an international war, followed by a catastrophic defeat such as that of Tsarist Russia in 1917, would provide the conditions for toppling a government within a matter of a few days or weeks. Hence the starting of an insurrection was likely to be separated by a long process from the later stage of its development culminating in the seizure of political power. For Che, not only should a revolutionary movement be built piecemeal, but also the launching of an insurrection is indispensable to the building of a revolutionary movement.

EVOLUTION OF THE FOCO STRATEGY

Che's preliminary sketch of the insurrectional foco or center in 'Social Projections of the Rebel Army' (January 1959) was filled in a year later in *Guerrilla Warfare* (Havana, 1960): first, popular forces can win a war against a regular army; second, it is not always necessary to wait for the conditions of revolution to develop because an insurrectional foco can create them; third, the most favorable terrain for armed struggle is the countryside (4).

Each of these precepts contradicted an established guideline of the communist parties in Latin America. The first challenged the belief that a revolutionary vanguard must establish political democracy and win a popular victory at the polls prior to a showdown with the military-bureaucratic apparatus. The second thesis challenged the dogma that revolutionaries must wait for the leadership of a

Marxist–Leninist party and for all the conditions of a revolutionary situation to be in existence before seizing arms and launching an armed struggle. The third thesis challenged the view that the most favorable terrain for waging an armed struggle lies in the cities where the proletariat is concentrated. Arguing that the revolutionary vanguard is least vulnerable in rural areas and in rugged country comparatively inaccessible to the regular army, Che concentrated on mobilizing the peasantry rather than the proletariat, through a program of agrarian reform.

Che set his first revolutionary objective when Arbenz fell: the forcible overthrow of Latin American dictators. Precedence was given to the most hated ones, Batista in Cuba, Trujillo in the Dominican Republic and Somoza in Nicaragua. In 'Social Projections of the Rebel Army' he warned that the Cuban Revolution was only the first of its kind which would place the dictators of Latin America on death row. He acknowledged with sarcasm, in a short article in *Verde Olivo* (Havana, April 1960), how the Cuban Revolution had poisoned the Latin American environment and threatened the sweet democracies of Trujillo and Somoza – the two immediate targets following the fall of Batista.

In its original version the foco was rated an effective strategy only against Latin American dictators typified by those in the Caribbean and in the 'banana republics' of Central America. As long as a government enjoys some form of popular consent, fraudulent or otherwise, Che argued, a foco will have difficulty in mobilizing popular support. The possibilities of legal struggle must have been exhausted or nullified by a government having seized or maintained power in violation of established laws. This proviso was subsequently revised on the assumption that legal avenues to social change had also been closed by most of the so-called democratic governments in Latin America.

The extension of the concept of the foco to apply to struggles against pseudo-democratic regimes was originally made in 'Cuba: Historical Exception or Vanguard?'. This essay points to underdevelopment as the common predicament of all Latin American countries and to the presence of objective conditions of revolution in all of them. The subjective conditions were to be created in the course of armed struggle (3). Thus the exhaustion of the possibilities for legal change had ceased to be regarded as peculiar to Latin American dictatorships.

Che's reformulation of his original model was vindicated with the suspension of Cuba from the Organization of American States (OAS) in January 1962 and by the Cuban government's response to that action. Only Mexico voted against the US-sponsored resolution; the democratic governments of Argentina, Brazil, Chile, Bolivia and Ecuador abstained. Furthermore, these governments joined the US in condemning Cuba's alignment with the USSR. In February the Cuban government responded with the Second Declaration of Havana – which Che called the Communist Manifesto of the Latin American Revolution. According to the Declaration, support for these US-sponsored resolutions constituted a renunciation of the Latin American people's right to self-determination, a sanctioning of US intervention in their internal affairs, and the virtual transformation of the OAS into a 'Yankee Ministry of Colonies'. The Latin American democracies had exposed themselves as tools of the native oligarchies, as traitors to national interests, and as enemies of social change. After backing the US against Cuba, they would not hesitate to solicit Yankee troops to repress a popular uprising in their own countries. In this perspective the known enemies of Cuba were also to be regarded as enemies of their own people.

In a speech to the Department of State Security, 'The Influence of the Cuban Revolution in Latin America' (May 1962), Che identified the viability of armed struggle with an entirely new set of factors: the extent of imperialist penetration, the geographical distance from the Yankee metropolis, and the influence of Cuban revolutionary ideas. Accordingly, he singled out not only Paraguay as ripe for revolution, but also countries with democratic and reformist governments: Peru, Ecuador, Colombia, Venezuela and Brazil. Noting the open hostility of most of these governments to the Cuban Revolution, he recommended that Cuba seek allies among their respective peoples.

He also called for Cuban encouragement and support of armed struggle in those countries, as part of Cuba's own strategy of self-defense.

The classic statement of Che's political-military strategy against pseudo-democratic regimes is contained in 'Guerrilla Warfare: A Method' (September 1963). With the exception of Cuba, all the Latin American governments are construed as oligarchical dictatorships, elected or not, because they are dominated by a bloc of the bourgeoisie and landowning class in each country (5). Appealing to Lenin's usage, Che identified those regimes with social dictatorships, whatever their form of government. It was not enough to overthrow Latin American dictators and to restore democracy, which was another form of oligarchical rule. Since oligarchical regimes attempted to rule with a democratic façade, Che argued, the task of revolutionaries was to unmask them. A strategy of polarization would oblige democratic governments to reveal their true colors and to disregard legal norms by resorting to violence. Che's strategy was to compel them to bow to popular movements for radical change or else, by repressing those popular movements, to initiate the phase of armed confrontation.

Che's strategy took a new turn in his December 1963 speech calling for solidarity with Vietnam. Aid to the National Liberation Front was imperative, he argued, because troops were being trained in Vietnam by the US which one day would be used against guerrilla movements in Latin America. Vietnam had become the great laboratory of Yankee imperialism for testing new methods of counterinsurgency as well as new weapons. For this reason the Vietnamese guerrillas were hailed as allies of the Cuban Revolution, as the front-line soldiers in a world struggle against imperialism through revolutionary fronts opened simultaneously in Asia, Africa and Latin America.

This version of the foco strategy took shape after the February 1965 bombing of North Vietnam and the dispatching of US troops to South Vietnam. The continental character of the Latin American Revolution had been acknowledged by Che as early as 1962, but it was not until his speech at the Afro-Asian People's Solidarity Organization in Algiers (February 1965) that he considered enlarging that organization to include revolutionary movements in Latin America. Partly through his initiative the Tricontinental was founded in Havana in January 1966 – a project hinted at in his Algiers speech. The meaning of proletarian internationalism, broached in his speech on Vietnam of December 1963, was also spelled out in Algiers: the disregard for geographical frontiers in the struggle against imperialism and the belief that a victory for any country against the common enemy would be a victory for all.

In Che's earlier strategies US imperialism was taken to be the main rather than the immediate enemy of the Latin American peoples. The immediate enemy was originally identified with Latin American dictatorships, subsequently reinterpreted to include pseudo-democratic regimes. Che's final strategy construed US imperialism to be both the main and the immediate enemy, and called for a direct confrontation with imperialism in every corner of the globe. By unleashing a direct military invasion of South Vietnam, followed by the invasion of Santo Domingo in April 1965, the US had discarded the earlier more cautious policy of indirect confrontation which it had applied in Guatemala against the Arbenz regime and in Cuba with the Bay of Pigs invasion of April 1961. The only effective response to this violation of national frontiers was to do likewise, to internationalize the revolution. Che prepared to counter US involvement in Vietnam with Cuban involvement in the former Belgian Congo (Kinshasa), where a similar revolutionary struggle was under way. Failing at this, he traveled to Bolivia in November 1966 with the objective of launching a new front in that country.

The final formulation of Che's strategy is contained in his 'Message to the Tricontinental' (April 1967). This strategy is no longer identified with the Cuban model but with the 'road to Vietnam' – the strategy most suited to South America (6). Acting through the Tricontinental, the Cuban vanguard of the Latin American Revolution had the task of creating a second and third Vietnam. The purpose of national liberation struggles was no longer the defeat of

Latin American dictators or the overcoming of pseudo-democracies, but the destruction of imperialism as a world system. Through the formation of international proletarian armies, and revolutionary committees synchronizing armed operations in neighboring countries, imperialism was to be challenged in a world confrontation. Elaborating on a theme from his Algiers speech, Che argued that the global struggle against imperialism could be successful only through a world socialist revolution. This was the high point of what might be called 'insurrectionary Guevarism'.

THE POSTINSURRECTIONARY PHASE

Outside Cuba, Guevarism has been influential mainly through the launching of insurrectional focos. Inside Cuba, it is its model of a Marxist–Leninist party that has become the principal agent of socialist construction. As the successor to the insurrectional foco, the vanguard party takes up the struggle for socialism and communism after the foco has waged a successful war of liberation. In effect, Guevarism is committed to a two-stage but continuous revolution in which the foco is the prime mover during the first stage and the Marxist–Leninist party is the prime mover during the second.

Nonetheless, Che left open the possibility that the dual task of a continuous revolution might be performed by a single organization. In an essay on 'The Marxist–Leninist Party' (1963), he conceived of the vanguard party not as an alternative to the foco, but as itself the political-military vanguard of the proletariat. Although not every political-military foco qualifies as a Marxist–Leninist party, no Marxist–Leninist party qualifies as a vanguard unless it has won that position through armed struggle. 'If the Marxist–Leninist party were capable of . . . becoming the vanguard of the people even before having overcome the stage of national liberation,' Che comments, 'then that party would . . . be able to confront the tasks of constructing socialism with more force and prestige among the masses.' In that event the vanguard party would have performed the dual historical mission of liberating its people through a war against the native oligarchy and imperialism, and then of constructing a new social order to take the place of the old.

The problem of how to combine the foco with a Marxist–Leninist party is tentatively dealt with in Che's 1964 prologue to the Cuban edition of General Vo Nguyen Giap's *People's War, People's Army* (Hanoi, 1961). In the Vietnamese model the guerrillas and the people's army are the mailed fists of a Marxist–Leninist party, which launches and directs the armed struggle. The revolutionary army consists not only of the people in arms, but also of the party in arms. The Vietnamese model is evidently more inclusive than the Cuban, but it is more difficult to apply.

The classic formulation of Che's conception of the Marxist–Leninist party is given in a speech 'On the Construction of the Party' (March 1963). In this speech he defined the two most important tasks of the vanguard party as the development of production and the intensification of political awareness (7). This thesis was reaffirmed in 'Socialism and Man in Cuba' (March 1965) in which he claimed that, to build communism, a new man must be created simultaneously with the material base (9) – a call for the parallel rather than the consecutive development of the economic and cultural revolutions in Cuba. This principle bears a striking resemblance to Che's first generalization concerning the insurrectional foco. Thus, although a vanguard party is not necessary to defeat a regular army, it is a *sine qua non* of overcoming capitalist relations of production.

In the same speech Che argued that the vanguard party does not have to wait on the development of economic conditions before initiating the transition to communism. As long as a sufficient minimum is present, objective conditions can be accelerated and the process of development shortened by using what Che calls 'catalysts'. In this way it is possible to skip intermediate stages and to begin the transition to communism prior to the consolidation of socialism. In effect, socialism and communism are the outcome not only of underlying economic antagonisms, but also of a vanguard party

27

accelerating and guiding the course of social transformation. As Che notes in 'The Marxist–Leninist Party', it is not necessary to wait for all the objective and subjective conditions to be given before proceeding to the construction of the new social order; the vanguard party can create them. There is an obvious resemblance between this principle and Che's second generalization concerning the insurrectional foco. This suggests that his theory of the vanguard party was deliberately modeled on the latter and that the insurrectional foco is thought of as the political embryo of a Marxist–Leninist party.

The fundamental appeal of such a party is to the organized proletariat rather than to the peasantry. In this light, it is noteworthy that Che's first reference to a dictatorship of the proletariat occurred in his essay 'On the Construction of the Party'. The foco had served as the political vanguard during the insurrectionary stage of the revolution; it had also been the principal agent of agrarian reform. The party, as the vanguard during the stage of building socialism, was to become the principal agent of Cuba's technological development. As Che comments in 'The Working Class and the Industrialization of Cuba' (June 1960), the revolutionary movement whose original aim was to mobilize the peasants through a program of agrarian reform subsequently shifted during its constructive stage to the principle of mobilizing the workers through a program of industrialization. There is an evident correspondence between this principle and Che's third generalization concerning the insurrectional foco. Although the ideal terrain of the foco is in the countryside, the principal locus of the party is in the cities.

The concrete tasks of the vanguard party are elaborated in Che's principal economic writings and summarized in his essay 'Socialist Planning: Its Significance' (June 1964). This essay reaffirms Lenin's thesis that the objective ties to international capitalism are weakest in underdeveloped countries and that subjective conditions there may contribute to a working-class movement capable of breaking the chain of imperialism at its weakest link. The strategy recommended by Che for overcoming economic dependence is the parallel and simultaneous construction of a technical economic base and the new man. Briefly, this is his answer to the question of how socialism can be built in a country colonized by imperialism, dependent on a single market and without basic industries of its own.

The model of socialist planning suited to underdeveloped countries, Che argued, is the so-called budgetary system of financing outlined in his essay of that title (*8*). This model represents a rejection of the Stalinist and post-Stalinist models of planning in favor of that outlined by Marx in the 'Critique of the Gotha Programme' (May 1875) and reaffirmed by Lenin in *State and Revolution* (Moscow, 1917). In the USSR capitalist relations of production have been overcome through the abolition of the private ownership of the means of production and the private appropriation of profits, dividends, interest and rent. Self-financed socialist enterprises compete with one another for profits, which serve as a measure of their economic performance. This is compatible with socialism, Che argues, but stops short of overcoming the mechanism of market relations as a condition of the transition to communism. According to the forementioned 'Critique', even the lowest stage of communism replaces market relations and the role of money with direct labor accounting in terms of standard man-hours. Although Che's model allows for commodity exchange in the case of consumer goods sold to the ultimate buyer, it excludes commercial transactions among industries and among the various branches of the same industry. Instead of paying interest on borrowed funds, consolidated enterprises are budgeted by a central planning agency with a view to increased productivity rather than profitability.

Che perceived that the role of the market combined with production for profit by socialist enterprises obscures efforts to calculate the labor content of commodities through the intermediary of their prices. In his June 1963 essay 'On the Costs of Production' and his February 1964 essay 'On the Budgetary System of Financing', he shows that poor countries cannot afford to be ignorant of the human costs of production in terms of labor. First, efforts to increase labor productivity cannot be accurately measured in terms of market prices alone, whose changes may reflect the operation of other variables including supply and demand. Second, reliance on the role of money tends to perpetuate the inequalities of wages and the fetishism of commodities inherited from capitalism, with the result that socialism becomes a fetter on the development of communist relations of production and the creation of a new man. Third, trade with socialist countries cannot be based on world market prices without perpetuating terms of trade unfavorable to exporters of primary goods, i.e., the underdeveloped countries.

While the budgetary system of financing aims at transforming capitalist into communist relations of production, Che's system of voluntary labor aims at transforming bourgeois human relations into communist relations. In a speech of January 1964, he argues that volunteer labor is less important in creating new wealth than in promoting a new attitude toward work. The objectives of volunteer labor are manifold: first, to transform drudgery into a socially shared revolutionary duty; second, to overcome the differences between intellectual and manual workers; third, to create cost-conscious citizens who, knowing what labor involves, seek to minimize waste. Volunteer labor is communist labor, a preview of work in a communist society performed without the inducement of material incentives.

The combined economic and educative tasks of the vanguard party were to be fulfilled through Che's budgetary system of finance and his system of voluntary labor. The objective of the budgetary system is to increase productivity by reducing costs; yet it also aims to educate the new man by reducing the scope of material incentives. The system of volunteer labor is designed to educate the new man; but its purpose is also to increase the volume of production. These two responses to underdevelopment contribute to defining Guevarism as a distinctive current within the Cuban Revolution, and for a brief period they enjoyed Fidel's support. However, the early abandonment of the budgetary system and the upgrading of material incentives in the 70s indicate that the Cuban Revolution subsequently charted a course of its own.

Guevarism emerged as a revolutionary trend distinct from Fidelism only after Che's assassination by US-trained Rangers in the jungles of south-eastern Bolivia. By the time of the August 1967 conference of the Organization of Latin American Solidarity (OLAS), the revolutionary's counterpart to the OAS, Che had already acquired a reputation as the new Bolívar engaged in the first stages of liberating South America through a second War of Independence. Yet it was not until his martyrdom on 8 October 1967 that Guevarist factions and groups of Guevarist devotees first appeared, most of which were subsequently repressed and physically eliminated during the wave of reaction and the mushrooming of military regimes during the early 70s.

Before October 1967 the partisans of the Cuban road to revolution were known as Fidelists. Régis Debray, the French philosopher of revolution and specialist in Latin American revolutionary struggles, was not alone in identifying the theory of the guerrilla foco with Fidelism or Castroism. Although acknowledging that its preconditions were first formulated by Che in *Guerrilla Warfare*, he took for granted that Guevara was principally a mouthpiece of the Cuban Revolution under Fidel Castro. In 'Castroism: The Long March in Latin America' (January 1965), Fidelism was described by Debray as the integration of Marxism–Leninism with the history of a continent unknown to Lenin. Again, in 'Problems of Revolutionary Strategy in Latin America' (July–August 1965), he identified the foco theory with Fidelism, a specifically Latin American adaptation of Leninism. As late as *Revolution in the Revolution?* (Paris, 1967), he continued to conceive of Che's contribution to the foco theory as auxiliary to that of Fidel, as an application on an international scale of the revolutionary strategy of which Fidel Castro, the leader of the Cuban Revolution, was the incarnation. At most, Debray anticipated that when Che again took up insurrectional work he would reappear as the undisputed leader of a new guerrilla movement, if not a separate and distinct revolutionary tendency.

Paradoxically, Che's death not only gave birth to Guevarism as a unique political-military strategy, but also gave renewed impetus to the forces for revolutionary change in Latin America. Efforts to liberate the continent were redoubled within days of Che's loss to the revolutionary movement. In Guatemala the Revolutionary Movement-November 13th (MR-13) under Yon Sosa and the communist-organized Rebel Armed Forces (FAR) under César Montes – among the most effective rural guerrilla movements on the continent during the 60s – issued a joint communiqué in which they set aside their programmatic differences for the example of unity set by Che in Bolivia. The death of a Titan, they declared, deserved a titanic response. Despite the political differences that had divided MR-13 and FAR since their formal rupture in March 1965, their October communiqué listed a series of eight points inspired by Che's thought and actions, on the basis of which the two movements were temporarily reunited in January 1968.

With Che's death the mythical side of his legacy threatened to eclipse momentarily the realistic features of his theory and practice. Portraits and banners of Che rather than Fidel were carried by the rebellious students who occupied the University of Nanterre and the Sorbonne during the French May Days of 1968. Within a year of his death, Che's exploits in Bolivia had captured the imagination of youth throughout the world, becoming second in importance only to the Vietcong as a symbol of the New Left. The Guatemalan FAR, the Chilean Movement of the Revolutionary Left (MIR), and the Argentine People's Revolutionary Army (ERP) recognized Che rather than Fidel as their symbolic commander, as did also the revived Bolivian Army of National Liberation (ELN) – guerrilla groups which survived the reversals of the late 60s and early 70s and continue to carry out military operations.

In view of the emergence of Guevarism as a separate revolutionary current its divisions and transformations must be distinguished from those peculiar to Che's own social and political philosophy. By 1968 his followers had begun to scrutinize his published works for justification of one or another self-styled form of Guevarism. The posthumous revolutionary movements bearing his name have thus added a new dimension to the corpus of Che's collected writings. At the same time, their varied positions on controversial issues are only partly reconcilable. Today, Guevarism is in conflict not only with Fidelism, but also with itself. Among the issues that presently divide Che's followers are differing interpretations of his strategy of the insurrectional foco, of the continental dimensions of Latin America's second War of Independence, of the comparative importance of urban and rural guerrilla warfare, and of armed support for broad fronts and popular governments.

VANGUARDIST VERSUS MILITARIST TENDENCIES

A crucial debate concerning Che's legacy revolves on the interpretation of his strategy of the insurrectional foco, more especially on the respective importance of its political-strategic and military-tactical components. In his manual on *Guerrilla Warfare* Che had endeavored to hold these factors in equilibrium by making military-tactical operations decisive within the context of a political-strategic struggle in which mass support was a *sine qua non* of victory against the repressive forces. However, as the Communist Party of El Salvador was among the first to perceive, Che subsequently abandoned his earlier strategy of providing fire-power for a mass movement of resistance, by making politics a continuation of war by other means and inverting the historic Leninist subordination of armed actions to the political struggle (*10*). In the effort to promote a Leninist conception of the armed struggle, the Salvadoran CP was thus obliged to repudiate the late in favor of the early Guevara.

That *Guevarismo* is not *foquismo* – *foquismo*, a term originated by the vanguardist tendency, indicates an exaggerated conception of the foco as a substitute for a vanguard party – is also a thesis of the Peruvian Revolutionary Vanguard (VR). The latter split with the Peruvian Movement of the Revolutionary Left (MIR) over precisely this issue of the relationship between the political vanguard and the cadres preparing for armed struggle (*11*). In a statement by the People's Revolutionary Army (ERP), an Argentine political-military organization with Trotskyist origins, a vanguard party is likewise recognized as the political core of the insurrectional foco (*12*). This tendency within Guevarism, according to which political-strategic considerations are primary and the launching of a foco is premature prior to the creation of the minimum conditions of a Marxist–Leninist party, is predicated on a vanguardist interpretation of Che's legacy.

The vanguardist tendency seeks an accommodation with Leninism by converting the foco into the armed fist of a political vanguard. As a precondition of launching an armed struggle, it gives precedence to the strengthening of a Marxist–Leninist party or to efforts to build such a party. One source of vanguardist interpretations consists of those established CP's, notably the Uruguayan and Salvadoran, whose leaderships have been directly inspired by the example of the Cuban Revolution. A second source includes those factions within the established CP's which have split to form independent parties committed to Che's early strategy of the foco, notably the originally but no longer promising Revolutionary Brazilian Communist Party (PCBR) and the increasingly ill-fated Revolutionary Communist Party (PCR) in Argentina. A third source of vanguardist interpretations of the foco are those pro-Guevarist movements concentrating on building Marxist–Leninist political organizations independent of both the old and new revolutionary CP's. Among these the most noteworthy examples are Peru's still viable Revolutionary Vanguard (VR) under Ricardo Letts ('Américo Pumaruna') and Brazil's now extinct Revolutionary Armed Vanguard (VAR-Palmares).

The most important single work in defense of the vanguardist tendency is João Quartim's *Dictatorship and Armed Struggle in Brazil* (London, 1971). A former militant of VAR-Palmares, Quartim considers the political role of the masses to be decisive in a revolutionary situation. The partisans of *foquismo* are criticized for concentrating on the demoralization of the repressive forces rather than on support for the day-to-day struggles of workers and peasants against their immediate exploiters, for rejecting systematic work in the mass movement and the trade unions, for underestimating the efficacy of political agitation and propaganda, and for reducing the organizational structure of the vanguard to armed groups alone. In support of the vanguardist thesis, Quartim underlines the need for a Leninist party directed to the political mobilization of workers and peasants as the vanguard class and the propelling force of the revolution.

The principal alternative to the vanguardist tendency is the *foquista* or predominantly militarist interpretation of the foco, inspired more by Che's later than by his early writings. In one of the first statements released by the Tupamaros (*14*), military action is said to create the political vanguard and the corresponding mass movement. The Tupamaros, whose origins can be traced to dissident youth elements in the Uruguayan Socialist Party, developed for a while the most important urban guerrilla organization on the continent. While conceding that the creation of a Marxist–Leninist party and a mass political movement is not wasted prior to launching an armed struggle, the Tupamaros claimed that such a struggle hastens and precipitates the organization of a vanguard party. Douglas Bravo, the political and military chief of the Armed Forces of National Liberation (FALN), which originated as an offshoot of the Venezuelan CP, also defends the role of a revolutionary party in promoting the struggle for national liberation (*13*). For him it is not a question of making the revolution with a party or without; the creation of a vanguard party is an indispensable condition of a successful revolution. In sharp contrast, the Army of National Liberation (ELN) in Bolivia issued a major policy statement on 4 August 1970 declaring that the revolution has no need of a party during the insurrectionary stage of the struggle, thus postponing the task of creating a party to the postinsurrectionary phase (*15*).

The extreme militarist interpretation by the Bolivian ELN shows the influence of Régis Debray in rejecting a vanguard party as less of an asset than a liability and in conceiving of the foco as a substitute for a party. His *Revolution in the Revolution?* set forth a new interpretation of the foco predicated on the premise that the Cuban Revolution had so spurred the forces of counter-revolution throughout the hemisphere that military rather than political factors had become decisive in launching an insurrection. Confronted with the occupation of rural areas by detachments of the regular army and with the building of new communications and transportation networks in those areas, the cadres preparing to launch a foco had little hope of escaping unnoticed by the government. Under these changed conditions, Debray noted, political work had become more difficult, as had the guerrilla's capacity to recruit new fighters. In this situation, he believed that political agitation should follow rather than precede military action, that the traditional relation between strategy and tactics should be inverted by launching armed operations as soon as they were militarily feasible, and that the foco should be prepared to survive initially without an urban supply network and support from the local population.

In an effort to overcome Debray's one-sidedness, the Tupamaros subsequently reconsidered the role of primarily political factors, among these the role of a vanguard party. A Tupamaro document, 'Party or Foco: A False Dilemma', dated August 1971 and published in *Los Libros* (Buenos Aires, November 1971), notes that the foco is a method of struggle, whereas a Marxist–Leninist party is a political apparatus. Consequently, revolutionaries are not compelled to choose between them, but are able to combine the two. First, an armed foco may contribute to the reconstruction, if not always the creation, of a vanguard party. Thus the July 26 Movement in Cuba and the Edgar Ibarra Front under Turcios Lima in Guatemala, which had originally belonged to MR-13 but split with it in March 1965, contributed to the reconstruction of the CP's in those countries. Second, a Marxist–Leninist party is capable of launching an insurrectional foco of its own, as did the Venezuelan CP in the form of Douglas Bravo's FALN. Third, a foco may be created parallel to and simultaneously with the building of a Marxist–Leninist party, as in the case of the Peruvian MIR.

Among other Guevarist-influenced movements that have tried successfully to overcome the vanguardist/militarist dichotomy, roughly along the lines recommended by the Tupamaros, is the Argentine ERP. Although the ERP is led by the Revolutionary Workers' Party (PRT), the party is incorporated in the ERP instead of the reverse. Far from being reduced to the armed fist of a political vanguard, the ERP is simultaneously a political and a military organization because it includes the PRT.

In Argentina the Peronist Montoneros, recruited from the youth section of the majoritarian Peronist Party named after its founder, the late President Juan Domingo Perón, have also successfully integrated the tasks of a political party with those of an insurrectional foco. Unlike the ERP, whose political and military leadership resides mainly in the PRT, the Montoneros have inverted this relationship between the foco and the party by providing the leadership for the Peronist Youth, the most important single youth organization in Argentina with the attributes of a political party. The advantage of this arrangement is that the political party, which serves the Montoneros as their mass political front, is nominally a legal organization. Thus the Montoneros are able to combine both legal and illegal forms of struggle, which has contributed to making them rather than the ERP the most important successor to the Tupamaros during the 70s.

DIFFERING INTERPRETATIONS OF A CONTINENTAL WAR OF LIBERATION

In his 'Message to the Tricontinental' Che added a new dimension to the continental struggle for liberation. He noted that an 'International of Crime and Treason' had already been organized under the mask of the OAS for the purpose of intervening in those countries where it might be necessary to prevent another Cuba. In response, Che favored an international confrontation in which the duty of every revolutionary was no longer to liberate his own country first, but to assist in the liberation of those countries currently in the throes of a revolutionary struggle. Although the initial plan for a Bolivian foco was presented to Che by Inti and Coco Peredo, the foco at Ñancahuazú was financed and launched from Cuban soil under Che's direct leadership. Thus from a war of national liberation patterned on the Cuban model, Che shifted to a strategy of initiating the liberation of other countries from beyond their own frontiers. Because of the analogy between Simón Bolívar's first War of Independence and Che's second War of Independence, Guevarists tend to refer to this new strategy as a Bolivarian one.

Debray, in a prison interview in the Uruguayan journal *Marcha* (Montevideo, 9 January 1970), questioned the viability of such a strategy, arguing that a fundamental factor underlying Che's failure in Bolivia was his underestimation of the role of nationalism in eliciting support for an insurrectional foco. Specifically, Debray maintained that each country must make its own national revolution under its own leaders, with the consequence that only the outcome of a revolution acquires continental dimensions. Because the guerrilla movement had been financed from Cuba and relied mainly on Cuban cadres for leadership, the Bolivian government was able to depict it as a foreign army of invasion. With this in mind Debray agreed substantially with Che's earlier strategy in 'Guerrilla Warfare: A Method': a continental struggle must emerge after national struggles for liberation, not before. Thus, the conditions of a continental struggle have to be created within each country, in expectation that a revolutionary war will act as a catalyst in neighboring countries.

The insistence on the continental character of the Latin American revolution and the need for a centralized command has also been disputed by Argentina's Revolutionary Armed Forces (FAR), as putting the cart before the horse. From having once subscribed to Che's continental strategy, FAR subsequently endeavored to nationalize it (20). Designed to form the Argentine contingent of Che's Bolivian foco, the original cadres of the FAR were prepared to return to Argentina under Che's orders once they had acquired military experience in Bolivia. Later they made plans to join Inti

Peredo's revived ELN, until the May 1969 'Cordobazo' (mass insurrection in the city of Córdoba) convinced them that the first task of liberation is a national rather than a continental one. By December 1970 FAR had opened discussions with the left wing of the Peronist Movement aimed at exploring the possible bases for unity. Finally, in May 1973, it issued its first statement in support of the new Peronist government of Héctor Cámpora, and in October merged organizationally with the powerful and popular Montoneros, a Peronist paramilitary group sharing a common position on armed struggle and the Argentine road to socialism.

Unlike the FAR, most of the Guevarist movements on the continent continued to subscribe to Che's continental strategy, of which there are at least four variations. First, the Venezuelan FALN under Douglas Bravo believed that Cuba should be the principal base for extending revolutionary war to the mainland, that a continental struggle requires a supreme or centralized command, and that the man most suited to direct a continental army of liberation was Fidel Castro, who had failed since 1969 to provide the requisite leadership (19). Second, the Bolivian ELN favored until 1973 a continental strategy in line with that of Che's original foco. The Bolivians were to assume the role of vanguard in South America under a single command, to which the various national organizations in neighboring countries were expected to contribute military cadres and financial assistance. Third, the Tupamaros convoked a 'Roundtable' in May 1970 at which a continental strategy was propounded based on regional co-ordinating committees or revolutionary juntas. The movements so represented would each have an equal voice. This proposal was originally backed by the Chilean MIR and later by the Argentine ERP and the Bolivian ELN, which agreed in a statement issued in Buenos Aires on 13 February 1974 to constitute a Revolutionary Co-ordinating Committee to synchronize armed operations in Bolivia and the Southern Cone (18). Fourth, under Carlos Marighela's leadership Brazil's once outstanding but now decimated Action for National Liberation (ALN) applied a continental strategy aimed at delivering Cuba from imperialist

39

encirclement, shifting the focus of armed struggle to Brazil, and provoking US intervention in the hope of making Brazil the first Latin American 'Vietnam'.

One of the most remarkable applications of Che's continental strategy was formulated by Ariel Collazo in 'Uruguay is no Exception' (May 1967). Collazo, the founder of the Uruguayan Revolutionary Movement (MRO), which has collaborated with the Tupamaros, argued on the basis of geopolitical considerations that Uruguayan militants should enlist in the revolutionary columns of neighboring Brazil and Argentina before attempting to liberate their own country (16). The geopolitical factors basic to this decision were the following: Uruguay's unfavorable terrain, with the absence of dense forests and mountains for launching rural focos; and the presence of reactionary military dictatorships in neighboring Brazil and Argentina, which would not hestitate to invade Uruguay in the event of a successful urban insurrection in Montevideo. Accordingly, Collazo recommended Che's continental strategy as the only viable one under these conditions, in the conviction that Uruguayan revolutionaries had little prospect of liberating their own country until after they had successfully liberated their more powerful neighbors.

The Tupamaros have been the principal disseminators of Che's continental strategy. On the basis of intelligence received by the Argentine secret services, the Buenos Aires newspaper *La Razón* (1 August 1970) reported that the Tupamaros had organized a Roundtable in May 1970 to discuss proposals for escalating and internationalizing armed struggles for liberation. The Tupamaros' Roundtable was said to have been attended by delegates of the Chilean MIR, the Bolivian ELN, the Colombian ELN, the Venezuelan FALN, the Brazilian ALN, the Argentine FAR, the Montoneros and their immediate predecessors in the Peronist Armed Forces (FAP), and the Uruguayan Revolutionary Armed Forces (FARO) founded by dissident members of Collazo's MRO. The Uruguayan socialist weekly *El Oriental* – a newspaper with close ties to the Uruguayan guerrillas – had reported on 24 June 1970 that such a Roundtable had been organized by the Tupamaros with the participation of Chato Peredo, the youngest of the three Peredo brothers and commander of the Bolivian ELN. Moreover, in a letter to the Tupamaros published in the Cuban newspaper *Granma* (1 August 1970), Chato Peredo acknowledged the assistance of that organization in launching a new Bolivian foco in the Teoponte region (*17*).

Further light on the continental strategy of the Tupamaros was provided by an official communiqué of 23 September 1973 by the armed forces of Uruguay, published by the Santiago de Chile weekly *Ercilla* (3–9 October 1973). The information indicated that a clandestine organization calling itself *La guacha chica*, supported by the Chilean MIR and directed by the Tupamaro leader Raúl Bidegain Gressing, was recruiting and training guerrillas in Chile for the purpose of launching an armed invasion of Uruguay. According to intelligence reports based on confessions by captured members of *La guacha chica* who had secretly returned to Uruguay from Chile, the guerrilla force of approximately five hundred members included not only exiled Uruguayans, but also Chileans, Bolivians, Peruvians and Argentines. Furthermore, in co-operation with the Chilean MIR, *La guacha chica* had allegedly tried to revive the armed struggle with a view to accelerating the transition to socialism in Chile.

COMPARATIVE IMPORTANCE OF URBAN AND RURAL GUERRILLA WARFARE

Che gave precedence to rural focos both in launching insurrections and in carrying them forward. Beginning with his manual on *Guerrilla Warfare*, he based this strategy on his distinction between favorable and unfavorable terrains for waging an armed struggle (*4*). Favorable terrains are those comparatively inaccessible to the repressive forces; unfavorable ones, those interlaced with roads and means of communication which permit the regular army to cordon off centers of subversion in encirclement-and-search operations. Rural guerrillas have the advantage of fighting on favorable terrain. Consequently, urban guerrillas are advised to play an auxiliary role, until the final phase of a war of national liberation when guerrillas in the countryside begin to converge on the cities.

As we have seen, in Che's writings the foco is a political-military commune for living together, fighting together and developing the new man. In this restricted sense, it is incompatible with an urban guerrilla organization in which the guerrillas fight together but live apart. Only in a loose sense does such an organization qualify as a foco, a rival of Che's strategy of rural-based guerrillas.

The first major break with Che's rural-based strategy was made by the Brazilian A L N and the Tupamaros. While agreeing with Che that rural guerrilla warfare is decisive and that the urban form of struggle is auxiliary to that in the countryside, Marighela contended that rural actions should be launched only after guerrilla operations in the cities (21). In the absence of financial and armed support from bases in other countries, he argued, urban guerrilla warfare alone can provide the means for waging armed struggle in the countryside. In that case, it is necessary to finance the rural struggle through bank expropriations and to obtain arms through raids on police posts and military installations. In effect, rural guerrillas cannot be established without prior armed actions by urban guerrillas.

At the same time, Marighela also rejected Che's strategy of the insurrectional foco. Using this term in its strict sense, he argued that a political-military organization for living as well as fighting together is hampered by lack of mobility. In opposition to the foco strategy, which is tied to a given region such as the Sierra Maestra in Cuba or the so-called 'Red Zone' of Che's operations in Bolivia, Marighela favored a war of movement that would introduce into rural struggles the kind of mobility characteristic of urban guerrilla operations – their rapid and periodic dispersal, regrouping and displacement from one battle zone to another. This meant that military cadres would be brought together only in pursuit of specific and momentary objectives; otherwise they would live apart and, like urban guerrillas, stop short of constituting a foco in the strict sense.

Only the Tupamaros, and the armed movements directly influenced by their example, favor the broad rather than the restricted application of this term to both urban and rural guerrillas. On the assumption that it is possible for urban-based focos to seize power independently of guerrillas in the countryside, there are at least two possible ways for these movements to co-ordinate armed operations. First, there is the option adopted by the Argentine Armed Forces of Liberation (FAL), an originally Leninist organization recruited from dissident elements in the Communist Youth, according to which the urban struggle is decisive, but the struggle in the countryside is indispensable. FAL stops short of subordinating the rural struggle to the urban form; both must be combined, presumably under a single command. Second, there is the option of the Tupamaros, that the struggle in the countryside is auxiliary to that in the cities and, furthermore, that it must be directed from the latter (23). These two strategies are to be contrasted to a third, that of the Zapatist Urban Front in Mexico, for which the urban and rural struggles are equally decisive and a single unified command is as yet unfeasible (22).

The strategy of the urban guerrilla first displaced that of rural guerrillas in Uruguay, a largely urbanized country. This strategy was then applied to Argentina and neighboring Chile. The centrality of rural guerrilla warfare is most viable in countries with a largely rural population and comparatively undeveloped urban centers – a point emphasized by Che in 'Cuba: Historical Exception or Vanguard?'. Actually, orthodox Guevarism survives mainly in Central America and the Andean countries – the most retrograde in Latin America – whereas neo-Guevarism, which assigns priority to urban guerrilla warfare, flourishes mainly in the modernized and predominantly urban populations of the Southern Cone.

In 1973 urban guerrillas made their first appearance in El Salvador, perhaps the most urbanized country in Central America. Because the countryside in El Salvador is generally unsuited to guerrilla warfare, orthodox Guevarists hope to develop rural focos in neighboring countries where the terrain is favorable. In an article written for *Tricontinental* (Havana, March–April 1969), the Salvadoran communist and exile, Roque Dalton, urges that rural focos be launched from the mountains of Guatemala, Honduras and Nicaragua, and extended to El Salvador when the struggle is sufficiently generalized throughout Central America. Salvadoran revolutionaries should participate in the insurrectionary struggles in those countries where conditions are favorable, he contends, and should launch an invasion of their own country only after having established liberated territories along its borders – a strategy closely resembling that of the Uruguayan MRO.

Faithful to the spirit if not always to the letter of Guevarism, neo-Guevarists have discovered loopholes in Che's writings, providing grounds for urban-based guerrilla warfare. In 'Cuba: Historical Exception or Vanguard?' Che acknowledged the possibility of victory by a popular rebellion with its guerrilla base in the cities. Nobody, he conceded, can object on theoretical grounds to the strategy of urban guerrillas; at most, it would be irresponsible for revolutionaries to underestimate the comparative vulnerability of urban cadres exposed to infiltration, treachery and capture by the repressive forces. With the door left open for divisions on this controversial issue, many of Che's followers have questioned the priority he assigned to rural guerrilla warfare.

THE RESPONSE TO BROAD FRONTS AND POPULAR GOVERNMENTS

There is no substitute for a foco, Che maintained, short of the destruction of the military-bureaucratic apparatus of the state. Should a populist movement be elected to power and resolve to push through a program of radical social reforms, then the most likely outcome is a military coup, following which new elections may be held after order is restored and the leaders of the deposed party have been sent into exile, to jail or to the grave. Should a nationalist junta seize power supported by so-called 'Nasserist colonels' and populist sectors of the army, then its reforms are likely to be resisted by other sectors of the military, culminating in a coup by one part of the army against another. In either case, popular governments have their hands tied according to Che: short of being overthrown by a counter-revolutionary coup, they tend to survive only through concessions to the oligarchy and reactionary sectors within the armed forces.

In the Dominican Republic such a military coup overthrew the popular government of Juan Bosch on 25 September 1963. Elected president with 60 per cent of the vote in December 1962, Bosch told a television audience shortly before the polls opened that his Dominican Revolutionary Party (PRD) could be expected not only to win the elections, but also to be overthrown by a military coup on the pretext that its reform program was a communist stratagem. Again, following a popular uprising in April 1965 supported by Bosch's party and a sector of the army under Colonel Francisco Caamaño Deno, the US marines intervened to restore 'order' and to reimpose an unpopular president on the country through fraudulent elections. A major statement by the Dominican CP (24) called for armed struggle against the new regime, but in the form of a broad front led by the constitutionalist and democratic forces under ex-President Bosch.

Not until the populist military juntas of General Velasco in Peru (1968–75) and of General Torres in Bolivia (1970–71) did Guevarist movements become divided on the issue of support for populist regimes. Although Che had no faith in such governments, some of his followers under Fidel Castro's influence eventually endorsed the Peruvian military junta as nothing less than the vanguard of the Peruvian Revolution. In an interview published in *Tricontinental* (27) Ricardo Gadea, the leader of the Peruvian MIR, and Héctor Béjar, the former commander of the Peruvian ELN, openly criticized Fidel on this score. Since his release from prison in January 1971, Gadea has refused to support the military junta on the grounds that it is opposed to workers' power and, instead of breaking the back of the oligarchs, favors their transformation into a new industrial bourgeoisie.

In contrast, Béjar abandoned his earlier opposition to the military regime, choosing to co-operate with it on the grounds that it had effectively mobilized the masses toward a revolutionary transformation of the country and the establishment of a rudimentary form of workers' self-management – an estimate of the junta also shared by Chile's late president, Salvador Allende. Even before his release from prison in 1971, Béjar was reconsidering his attitude to the junta. Thus in his interview in *Tricontinental*, he acknowledged the fundamental strategic problem of steering a middle course between unconditional opposition to and unconditional support for populist governments in Latin America. He reflected that in the case of Perón's first and second labor governments (1946–55), the left-wing opposition had played into the hands of the oligarchy with its very opposition, whereas the Guatemalan left had shared the fate of Arbenz's government (1950–54) by having become its principal apologist. With these examples before him, Béjar opted for a third position, that of critical support for the Peruvian junta – a middle road presumably avoiding the mistakes of the Argentine and Guatemalan experiences.

The Torres regime went beyond its Peruvian counterpart in bending to mass pressures and in countenancing a Popular Assembly or system of dual power – the first of its kind in the Americas. The government's opening to the left was not enough, however, to neutralize the ELN. In a communiqué dated 10 October 1970, the ELN repudiated the populist military junta because of the historic lesson provided by every populist government on the continent: the failure to smash decisively the power of the oligarchy and the reactionary military forces (*28*). Among the examples cited were the governments of Perón in Argentina, Vargas in Brazil, Arbenz in Guatemala, Bosch in the Dominican Republic and Paz Estenssoro in Bolivia.

Following the inauguration of the Popular Assembly on May Day 1971, the ELN continued its armed operations for the purpose of building its own forces. Hardly was the first meeting of the Assembly over when ELN cadres abducted the German-born industrialist, Johnny von Bergen, demanding $50,000 in ransom. In an ELN communiqué of 8 May 1971 explaining this action to the Bolivian people, the kidnapping was justified as a means of financing a revolutionary apparatus capable of eliminating fascism before it reached the government. Since the government had yet to eliminate centers of actual and potential counter-revolution within the armed forces, the ELN announced its intentions of developing a counter-power of its own – a strategy comparable to that of the Argentine ERP following Perón's accession to the presidency in September 1973.

The responses of Guevarist political-military organizations to the electoral struggles of Chile's Popular Unity coalition in 1969–70 and of Uruguay's Broad Front in 1970–71 also indicate differences over strategy. Although the Chilean MIR openly repudiated the candidates of the Christian Democratic and National parties in the elections of 1970, it did not endorse publicly the candidacy of Salvador Allende or his socialist-communist united front. Moreover, its subsequent critical support of Allende lasted only until August 1973, when the MIR repudiated the compromising policies of the government and began building an independent revolutionary bloc aimed at encouraging expropriations and developing workers' power (*29*). In contrast, the Tupamaros endorsed the far more heterogeneous Broad Front in the Uruguayan elections of November 1971, a popular front dominated by deserters from the established political parties rather than by socialists and communists, who represented a definite minority. Otherwise, the MIR and the Tupamaros concurred in distrusting the revolutionary potential of a victory at the polls, while concentrating on building their own organizations (*26*).

The electoral victory of the Peronist Movement in March 1973 and the inauguration of President-elect Cámpora in May deepened the divisions among Argentine Guevarists along lines roughly parallel to those in Peru. The ERP agreed at most to a conditional truce with the new government, whereas the FAR offered to collaborate. In a FAR document dated May 1973, the following reasons were cited for such a strategy: first, the revolutionary sectors of Peronism represent a minority at the policy-making level with an opportunity of winning a hegemonic position, itself the best guarantee for the uninterrupted development of the liberation process in Argentina; second, the Peronist and Guevarist paramilitary organizations lack sufficient fire-power to defeat the regular army, so that elementary prudence counsels limited struggles and the avoidance of a showdown until the guerrillas have a force capable of winning (*25*). In sharp contrast, the

ERP called for the escalation of armed conflict against the reactionary armed forces and the multinational corporations. It is still too early to assess the comparative advantages and disadvantages of these alternative strategies. At most, it is worth noting that, after the calling of new elections in September 1973 which returned Perón to the presidency, his government and its successor under Isabel Perón waged an all-out campaign against the ERP aimed at exterminating the more orthodox Guevarists in Argentina.

The impact of Guevarism on Third World liberation movements

The influence of Guevarism is not confined to Latin America. Kim Il Sung, the premier of North Korea, has spoken of Che's importance to revolutionary movements throughout the Third World. In North Vietnam the two principal themes of philosophical research in the early 70s were the struggle against neocolonialism and the education of the new man, at least partly inspired by Che's influence. The Ceylonese insurrection of 1971 had a strong Guevarist contingent, and in the Middle East the works of Debray have directly influenced Palestinian terrorist organizations, notably Black September. In Africa the influence of Guevarism is less evident, despite Che's involvement in the Congo. His influence has been greater on the national liberation movements of 'Third World' peoples within the First World, on the Irish Republican Army, the Quebec Liberation Front and the Black Panthers in the United States. Yet only in Latin America have Guevarist tendencies assumed a leading or decisive role on the left.

Originally, the guerrilla movements on the mainland were influenced less by Che's manual of *Guerrilla Warfare* than by the historic example of the July 26 Movement. Fidel Castro was the first to cause a rupture between the revolutionary youth section of a social democratic party – the Cuban People's Party (Orthodox) – and the reformist politics of its leaders. His break with that party in March

1956 became the model for subsequent splits by the youth sections of the corresponding social democratic parties in Peru in 1959 and Venezuela in 1960. Thus the emergence of the first Movements of the Revolutionary Left (MIR's) in Peru and Venezuela are to be credited less to Che's influence than to Fidel's.

Since 1967, however, when Guevarism emerged as a separate revolutionary force, it has had a major influence on the younger generation of the established CP's, on Latin American Trotskyists and on dissident cadres of the left-wing Socialist parties. At the same time other movements have adopted a Guevarist strategy, while remaining faithful to their political origins. Once the Tupamaros established the viability of urban guerrillas, militant anarchists began joining that organization. The convergence of left-wing Peronists with Guevarist positions began during the early 60s and is today stronger than ever. Finally, a new Christianity emerged under the influence of the guerrilla-priest Camilo Torres. Not only in Colombia, but also in Chile, Uruguay and Argentina, partisans of Camilo Torres have broken with the established Christian Democratic parties in favor of a Guevarist alternative.

A TREND WITHIN THE CUBAN REVOLUTION

For a brief period during the early and middle 60s, Fidel Castro was willing to experiment with Che's novel economic strategy. Thus, in a 1966 May Day speech, he identified the uniqueness of the Cuban road with the parallel construction of socialism and communism (*30*). In so doing, he repudiated the Soviet model of building communism only after the consolidation of socialism. Using Soviet terminology, Fidel acknowledged that the first stage of postcapitalist society is characterized by the survival of material incentives, commodity production, the role of money, production for profit, and a system of socialist enterprises linked by market relations. Nonetheless, parallel to the socialist sector, Fidel called for the creation of a communist sector free of the remnants of the old order, a sector characterized by voluntary labor and the development of a new attitude toward work.

49

In effect, Fidel opted for a Guevarist model of creating a new man parallel to and simultaneously with a new technological base (9).

Although Fidel expressed reservations concerning Che's system of consolidated enterprises, his speeches reflect the influence of the most important Guevarist themes. Like Che, he believed that communism is possible prior to the creation of material abundance and that, with contemporary conditions of underdevelopment, the elimination of poverty depends on voluntary sacrifices and communist political awareness. Extreme deprivation requires extreme measures to combat it: communism may be superfluous to the creation of wealth in the advanced countries, Fidel acknowledged, but is a necessary condition of opulence in the underdeveloped ones. In a speech of 13 March 1968 launching the revolutionary offensive against small proprietors and independent businessmen, he justified the closing of bars and the legislation against street vendors on the grounds that a poor country must invest its last penny for development and mobilize all its energies in that endeavor. People can shine their own shoes; shoe-shine boys are more effectively employed in agriculture or industry. Everyone must be obliged to work – hence the Cuban law against loafers – but in socially useful occupations.

Under these conditions, top-priority work creates products which re-enter the cycle of production or otherwise contribute to earning foreign exchange for the purchase of such products. An underdeveloped country must take short cuts to overcome the distance separating it from the more developed ones. This requires not only maximum utilization of all material and human resources, but also their allocation to top-priority employments. Petty commerce may offer more material incentives than the labor of a factory operative; but then, as Fidel notes, so does imperialism.

THE INFLUENCE OF GUEVARISM ON THE ESTABLISHED CP's

During the early 60s the Venezuelan and Guatemalan Communist parties, under the generalized influence of the Cuban Revolution, formally organized and launched guerrilla movements in their respective countries. Owing to differences with their party leaders accentuated by the Guevarization of Cuban domestic and foreign policy, these movements later declared their independence of the established CP's. The leadership of the Venezuelan FALN was reorganized by Douglas Bravo in December 1965. Bravo was subsequently suspended from the Politburo in March 1966 and expelled from the Party in April 1967. In an interview in the Sierra del Falcón in June 1967 published in a French collection, *Avec Douglas Bravo dans les maquis vénézuéliens* (Paris, 1968), he acknowledged his complete agreement with the tricontinental strategy sketched by Che in April of that year – a strategy that FALN continued to apply throughout the early 70s. Following Che's death in October, the Guatemalan FAR under the command of César Montes reiterated its allegiance to Guevarism, and in January 1968 followed Bravo's example by ceasing to be an armed detachment of the Guatemalan Workers' Party. As evidence of the prevailing Guevarist tendency within the FAR, its communiqué of 21 January 1968 not only announced its independence, but also concluded with a declaration of loyalty to the memory, example and leadership of Che Guevara (*31*).

The influence of Guevarism is also evident in the armed actions of national liberation fronts organized by CP cadres independent of their party's direction. Marighela resigned in December 1966 from the Executive Committee of the Brazilian CP over the issue of armed struggle versus a strategy of support for the so-called rede-mocratization of Brazil. In a letter to Fidel dated 18 August 1967 he affirmed his allegiance to the OLAS, and in February 1968 he began preparations for armed resistance (*33*). The formal break with the Party occurred in 1968. On the basis of the Party's apparatus in São Paulo headed by Marighela, the ALN arose for the express purpose of continuing the struggle begun by Che in Bolivia.

The Sandino Front of National Liberation (FSLN) was formed in 1962 by cadres who had become disillusioned with peaceful efforts at reform by the Nicaraguan Socialist Party, i.e., the Nicaraguan CP. Under the leadership of Carlos Fonseca Amador, later founder and president of the FSLN, these cadres had begun in 1959 to wage a guerrilla struggle against the Somoza dictatorship (*32*). The break with the Party was formalized in 1962, after which the FSLN began to develop a politics and strategy modeled along Fidelist and Guevarist lines.

Some Communist parties chose to modify their strategy of peaceful and legal struggles by incorporating special features of Guevarism. The first to do so was the Uruguayan CP, followed by the Communist Party of El Salvador – countries similar in size, in terrain, and in the demographic distribution of their populations. By the middle of 1967 and in response to Che's Bolivian campaign, the Uruguayan Communists had reversed their earlier support for the peaceful road to socialism, convinced that in Latin America the majority of national liberation struggles would take the form of armed insurrections and guerrilla wars. Although the new strategy did not preclude legal work, it was tantamount to support for the armed struggle in Bolivia and to preparations for an eventual armed confrontation in Uruguay. In an epilogue to the Salvadoran edition of Che's *Bolivian Diary* (San Salvador, 1968) entitled 'We Must Learn the Larger Lessons of Che's *Diary in Bolivia*', the Political Commission of the Salvadoran CP affirmed its support of guerrilla warfare where people can be persuaded that legal forms of struggle are useless (*10*). Claiming that the peaceful road had become a dead end for Latin American revolutionaries, the epilogue also criticized Debray's interpretation of Guevarism for its putschist conception of the armed struggle and its view of politics as an auxiliary of military actions. These actions were to be seen instead as a continuation of politics by other means.

In some instances the CP leaderships became penetrated by Guevarist cadres, resulting in right- or left-wing splits from the established party. In 1967 the Honduran CP opted for an immediate strategy of guerrilla warfare (*34*). In response, the right wing organized a rival CP which, despite its minority status, was then recognized by Moscow as the sole representative of the Communists in that country. In Argentina and Brazil, where the left wings of the

CP's constituted minorities rather than majorities, splits also occurred over the question of armed struggle. On 6 January 1968 dissidents from the Argentine CP founded the Communist Party of Revolutionary Recovery, later renamed the Revolutionary CP (PCR) (35). And in April of the same year the Revolutionary Brazilian CP (PCBR) was founded by such 'old Communists' as Mario Alves, Jacob Gorender and Apolonio de Carvalho – and this too was a party committed to preparations for armed struggle.

THE GUEVARIZATION OF LATIN AMERICAN TROTSKYISM

Che's influence on Latin American Trotskyism can be traced as far back as 1960. In that year Che was interviewed in Havana by two Trotskyists from Argentina, the Spanish exile José Martorell and the Peruvian exile Ricardo Napurí (Silvestre Condoruma). As reported by Gonzalo Añi in his *Secret History of the Guerrillas* (Lima, 1967), Martorell returned to Argentina where he persuaded Daniel Pereyra and other Trotskyist militants of the viability of the insurrectional *foco* and of the need to develop armed support for Hugo Blanco's peasant unions in Peru (36). The long-range effect of the Guevarist trend initiated by Martorell was the expulsion of the anti-Guevarists from the PRT in 1968 and the launching of the ERP in 1970.

Returning to Peru, Napurí joined the MIR, from which he separated in 1965 to found the Revolutionary Vanguard (VR). Unlike the MIR, VR was committed to the development of the minimum conditions sufficient for a Marxist–Leninist party prior to the launching of armed struggle. In an interview with the author in a Lima hotel room in February 1970, Napurí claimed to have spent more than a hundred hours with Che over a period of six months, as a result of which he adopted a modified *foco* strategy combining mass political actions and guerrilla warfare (37). As in the case of Martorell, Napurí's encounter with Che led to the first rapprochement between Trotskyism and Guevarism in Latin America.

53

Trotskyism is distinguished as a revolutionary movement by its commitment to the theory and strategy of permanent revolution. The theory claims to establish the dependence of a democratic revolution in underdeveloped countries on a parallel and simultaneous proletarian revolution. Its basic premise is that the democratic and national liberation struggles in backward colonial and semicolonial countries cannot be completed without making deep inroads into the rights of property. Relying on the experience of the Russian Revolutions of 1905 and 1917 and of the abortive Chinese Revolution of 1925–7, Trotskyists argue that democratic revolutions in underdeveloped countries tend to be aborted unless they follow a socialist course. In effect, a democratic revolution that is not a permanent or continuing one is self-defeating. Strategically, Trotskyists take this to mean that it must be led by the proletariat and by a Marxist–Leninist vanguard party. Although most Guevarists implicitly accept Trotsky's theory of permanent revolution, they reject its strategy. Accordingly, they deny both that the democratic revolution must be led by the proletariat rather than by the peasantry, and that the insurrectional foco must be subordinated to a Marxist political party.

The Guevarization of Latin American Trotskyism is evident mainly among the parties affiliated to the Fourth International (Unified Secretariat), notably in its Bolivian and Argentine sections. There are in fact three Fourth Internationals distinguished by the names of their respective secretariats or directing committees: the Unified Secretariat or largest, the International Secretariat and the International Committee. In Bolivia the Revolutionary Labor Party (POR-*Combate*), under the leadership of Hugo González, was prevented by the Bolivian CP in 1966–7 from linking up with Che's ELN. Not until 1969 were members of González' group recruited individually by the ELN, following a political agreement with Inti Peredo, the ELN's second commander. In 1970 the revived ELN under Chato Peredo also included a Trotskyist contingent. At the same time, POR-*Combate* retained its organizational independence of the ELN. Faithful to its Trotskyist origins, in a May Day message in 1971 it called for an immediate struggle for socialism against the populist government of General Torres on the ground that the government's reformist strategy was providing fuel for the counter-revolution (*38*).

The largest and most influential of the Latin American sections of the Fourth International (Unified Secretariat) was the Argentine PRT and its fighting organization, the ERP, clandestinely created at the Party's fifth Congress in July 1970. From the beginning the ERP hailed Guevara as its symbolic commander. It also acknowledged the important urban modifications of the foco strategy introduced by Marighela's ALN and the Tupamaros. Fraternal relations were established with these movements and the FSLN of Nicaragua, the Chilean MIR and the POR-*Combate* in Bolivia.

Under Guevarist influence, the PRT-ERP began to reject the 'Trotskyist' label. This led to a three-way split in February 1973, from which emerged two side-currents: the ERP-August 22nd, opposed to continued membership in the Fourth International and in favor of a united front with the left-wing sectors of the Peronist Movement; and the ERP-Red Faction, committed to a more orthodox line and the necessity of a world revolutionary party. For a while the main body of the ERP chose to remain within the Fourth International, but for the express purpose of 'proletarianizing' it. Actually, the ERP had already converged on Che's politics and strategy and was no longer unilaterally tied to the Trotskyist tradition, which accounts for its final break with the Fourth International in June 1973 (*39*).

GUEVARISM AMONG DISSIDENT SOCIALISTS

Next to the established CP's and the Trotskyist parties, Guevarism has had a major impact on militants of the reconstructed Socialist parties in Latin America. Among those parties that have severed their ties to European social democracy, the most important have been the Uruguayan and Chilean. In the early 60s both parties came under the influence of the Cuban Revolution, but this turn toward the left did not occur soon or fast enough for the younger generation. By 1965 independent movements for revolutionary action had been organized by disaffected militants from both parties: the Uruguayan Movement of National Liberation (Tupamaros) and the Chilean Movement of the Revolutionary Left (MIR).

The genesis of the Tupamaros can be traced to the failure of the Artigas Sugar Workers' Union (UTAA) to get the central government to enforce social legislation directed at the sugar companies. Founded in 1961 by the Socialist Party militant, Raúl Sendic, the Union in 1962 organized a march of caneworkers and their families, who walked 600 kilometers from Artigas to Montevideo to publicize their grievances. Disillusioned by the march's reception, the leaders subsequently opted for a strategy of armed self-defense. This led to the assault on the Swiss Colony Rifle Club in July 1963, from which Sendic's group seized their first automatic rifles.

During 1963–4 Sendic's followers were recruited from militant cadres of the Socialist Party under a secret agreement with the Party's leadership. Only in 1965 did the Tupamaros emerge as an independent armed organization no longer tied to the Party, although they had yet to come under the influence of Guevarism as a distinctive revolutionary trend. By 1968 they were openly acknowledging its influence (*41*). In 'Thirty Questions to a Tupamaro' (June 1968), the first public declaration of their views, they accepted Che's strategy of the insurrectional foco in its final or tricontinental form, while adapting it to an urban environment (*14*).

In August 1965 Chile's MIR was organized by dissident elements from the Socialist Party, but with the participation of high-ranking cadres from two of Chile's Trotskyist parties. Despite its nominal resemblance to the Venezuelan and Peruvian MIR's, it was a Marxist–Leninist movement from the start. Its principal spokesman and chief theoretician was Miguel Enríquez, who, like Sendic, was a former Socialist. Again like Sendic, he left the SP in 1964, when it became apparent to him that his party's strategy was basically reformist rather than revolutionary. From the beginning, the MIR showed evidence of Trotskyist influence in its sharply defined criticism of the revisionist governments of eastern Europe, its rejection of any alliance with the petty bourgeoisie, and its option for an immediate socialist revolution. Not until 1968 did it begin the transition to armed struggle on the basis of an urban guerrilla strategy borrowed mainly from the Tupamaros.

The Guevarization of the MIR can be traced to its decision to support the continental strategy of 'many Vietnams' outlined by Che in his 'Message to the Tricontinental'. A formal statement of support by the Political Secretariat was first published in the MIR's theoretical organ *Estrategia* (Santiago de Chile, June 1967). In view of direct US military intervention in Santo Domingo and Vietnam, the MIR noted that the US had effectively notified the Latin American people that it would not permit the installation of new anti-imperialist or prosocialist governments in the hemisphere. For this reason, MIR rejected as illusory the prospect that the Chilean Socialist and Communist parties could constitute a popular government through a victory at the polls. Allende was permitted by the US and by the Chilean military to govern temporarily – at least until the coup of September 1973 – but the MIR was not mistaken in its forecast. The immediate survival of the Popular Unity government was attributed to its policy of concessions to the established political parties. Although the MIR gave its critical support to Allende after the elections, it withdrew that support in August 1973 on the ground that he had capitulated to the combined forces of the military and the bourgeois opposition in Congress. In an editorial in its newspaper *El Rebelde* (14–20 August 1973) the MIR reaffirmed its Guevarist foundations, declaring that the only way remaining for the working class was to rely on its own forces: first, by resisting the government's decision to return certain enterprises to their former owners; second, by developing an instrument of combat capable of enforcing workers' control (*29*).

THE CONVERGENCE OF ANARCHISM ON GUEVARISM

The convergence of militant anarchism on Guevarism has been encouraged by the priority Che assigned not only to violent confrontation with the state, but also to the propaganda of the deed. Like Bakunin, Che favored a political-military confrontation on an international scale. Not for nothing did he note in his *Bolivian Diary* (Havana, 1968) that the Czech Communists had publicly condemned his 'many Vietnams' strategy, while likening him to a 'new Bakunin'. Che's criticism of the established CP's recalls in fundamental respects Bakunin's 'Letters to a Frenchman on the Present Crisis' (September 1870), which anticipated some of the basic elements of Che's strategy of the insurrectional foco. A social revolution can be launched without a prior political revolution because no army in the world, Bakunin argued, however strong and well equipped, can overcome irregular fighting units supported by the masses. Second, the most powerful and irresistible form of propaganda consists of deeds, which inspire trust and stir the people to revolt. And third, revolutions cannot be exported from the cities to the countryside, but must be germinated independently in rural areas, through a strategy that will satisfy the peasant's hunger for the land by destroying the power of the landlords.

During the 60s and early 70s the most outstanding spokesman for the Bakuninist current within Latin American anarchism was the Spanish Civil War veteran and exile, Abraham Guillén. He was Latin America's first strategist of urban guerrilla warfare – a strategy directly incorporated by the Tupamaros and urban guerrillas in both Brazil and Argentina. His most influential work, *Strategy of the Urban Guerrilla* (Montevideo, 1966), favored the parallel development of urban and rural focos throughout the River Plate basin, the priority of urban over rural guerrillas in countries with a predominantly urban population, the choice of a favorable population rather than a favorable terrain for waging an armed struggle, and an urban strategy based on the principle that guerrillas should fight together but live apart in order to escape detection.

In January 1968 Guillén published an Introduction to the Uruguayan edition of Che's *Guerrilla Warfare* (Montevideo, 1968), which directly subscribed to Che's first two principles of the insurrectional foco: that a handful of politically aware and determined men can defeat the armies of the oligarchy; and that the conditions of a revolutionary situation can be created through armed actions provided one knows where, how, with what, and for what an insurrectionary foco should be launched (*42*). Guillén agreed with Che that a foco rather than a political party is the agent *par excellence* of armed actions, and that a vanguard party should emerge from the foco rather than the reverse. However, he rejected Che's third principle – that the focus of armed struggle should be in the countryside. The defeat of Che's guerrillas in Bolivia was attributed by Guillén to this mistaken dictum.

Guillén's adaptation of Guevarism is further evident in a chapter on 'The Theory of the Insurrectional Foco' from his *Challenge to the Pentagon* (Montevideo, 1969). There Che's concept of a favorable terrain is redefined to include cement jungles which, although accessible to the enemy, provide hiding places in the same way as real jungles. Guillén argues that Che's first and second principles of guerrilla warfare require for their success not only a favorable terrain, but also a favorable population organized into paramilitary cadres on a territorial basis, and a vulnerable enemy confronted by a numerically superior and hostile front of the oppressed classes. The enemy is most vulnerable, he observes, in countries where military dictators have dissolved congress and outlawed the opposing political parties. Thus, returning to Che's original model of the foco (*4*), Guillén argues that Latin American dictatorships rather than representative regimes afford the best prospects for an insurrectionary struggle.

THE CONVERGENCE OF PERONISM ON GUEVARISM

Guevarism has also been successful in converting the left wing of the Peronist Movement to a revolutionary strategy against imperialism. From its beginning, the Peronist Movement consisted of an alliance between young nationalist military officers and the non-Marxist wing of organized labor in Argentina. Fathered by Colonel Juan Domingo Perón, the popularly elected president of Argentina from 1946 to 1955, it is distinguished from other revolutionary nationalist movements on the continent by virtue of its philosophy of justicialism or social justice. In the effort to moderate the difference between an irresponsible individualism and a suffocating collectivism, the Peronist philosophy favors a so-called 'third position' intermediate to capitalism and communism. This third position is tantamount to a form of non-Marxist socialism adapted to Argentine national traditions. There is an element of demagogy in the use of the nationalist and socialist labels. The capitalist system is preserved and modernized, but the bourgeoisie are not allowed to rule. Instead, they are replaced by a government typically under the control of a military and political bureaucracy, but with strong labor representation. The Peronist program of 'political sovereignty, economic independence and social justice' is a program of social reforms rather than revolution. Nonetheless, with Perón in exile and the Peronist Movement officially banned from 1955 to 1973, the Peronist program was given a revolutionary interpretation by the Movement's increasingly assertive and pro-Guevarist left wing.

In June 1960 there was a meeting in Havana between Che and three ranking members of the Peronist Movement including Perón's personal representative, John William Cooke. This meeting culminated in a Guevara–Perón pact aimed at overthrowing the government of President Arturo Frondizi, which had been elected under conditions in which the Peronist or majority party had been barred from running its own candidates. The pact led directly to the establishment of guerrilla training centers in Argentina under Cuban instructors – discovered and dismantled by government forces in July 1961.

Cooke's proclivity for armed struggle was evident even before this top-level conference with Che. During the months immediately preceding the fall of Perón in September 1955, Cooke had foreseen the imminence of a military coup and begun preparations to resist it. A former collaborator with Abraham Guillén on the review *De*

Frente (Buenos Aires, 1954–5), Cooke sought his advice in organizing clandestine guerrillas, as an alternative to the popular militias openly demanded by the trade unions. The Cooke–Guillén plan was vetoed by army officers loyal to Perón on the ground that the guerrillas would interfere with the operations of a unified military command. Not until December 1959, in response to the victory of the Cuban guerrillas over Batista, did a group of Cooke's followers launch an insurrectional foco in the province of Tucumán, in which Guillén served as chief of staff. This movement, known as the Uturuncos after the name of its commander, disbanded after a series of tactical successes and was not heard of again.

Another revolutionary Peronist, the legendary Joe Baxter, collaborated with the Uturuncos from Buenos Aires and then, under Cooke's political influence and Guillén's strategy of guerrilla warfare, launched the first Peronist urban guerrilla actions against the Polyclinic Bank of Buenos Aires in August 1963 – about the same time that the Peronist Jorge Masetti was preparing to launch a second rural foco in north-west Argentina under instructions from Che Guevara. Baxter was also personally responsible for the transformation of the Revolutionary Nationalist Movement (Tacuara), of which he was a leader, from a semifascist, anti-Semitic, right-wing nationalist organization into a left-wing movement committed to Cooke's revolutionary line. Following the arrest in February 1964 of five members of Baxter's organization for complicity in the hold-up, the Tacuara was obliged to go underground. Although Baxter and three other Peronists escaped to Montevideo, where they gave military instruction to the Tupamaros and collaborated in further bank raids, the Tacuara virtually ceased to operate on Argentine soil.

The most important successor to the Tacuara, forcibly disbanded in February 1964, was the Peronist Revolutionary Movement (MRP) founded in August of that year. It was the MRP which indirectly gave birth to both the Peronist Armed Forces (FAP) in Tucumán in 1968 – a successor to the Uturuncos – and to the Montoneros who launched armed actions in the federal capital in May 1970 with the kidnapping, trial and killing of Argentina's ex-president, Pedro

61

Eugenio Aramburu. In April 1971 the MRP reaffirmed its commitment to guerrilla warfare in a statement published in *Cristianismo y Revolución (44)*. In the same context, it called for a unified political-military front against the dictatorship, for the integration of the day-to-day struggles of organized labor with those of students and revolutionary intellectuals against their common enemy, and for the intensification of the revolutionary war in collaboration with factory and neighborhood commandos organized by the workers.

Next to Cooke, the most important Peronist leader to adopt a Guevarist line was Raimundo Ongaro, Secretary of the Graphics' Union and head of the left-wing majority of the General Confederation of Labor (CGT) from 1968 to 1970, calling itself the 'CGT of the Argentines'. Under his leadership the CGT of the Argentines identified imperialism and its native supporters as the principal enemy, and organized an anti-imperialist front of workers, petty bourgeois, students and various guerrilla organizations (43). During the first 'Cordobazo' in May 1969, Ongaro emerged as a national hero in the struggle to bring down the military regime. But in June the leader of the rival right-wing labor federation and former head of the CGT, Agusto Vandor, was assassinated by left-wing Peronists, following which Ongaro was arrested, a state of siege proclaimed by the military, and the principal unions affiliated with the CGT of the Argentines placed under government control. When pressure from Perón led to the reunification of the CGT in 1970 it was not Ongarism that triumphed, but a new centrist leadership under José Rucci. Later, in September 1973, Rucci suffered the same fate as Vandor, dying from an assassin's bullet.

CHE, CAMILO AND THE NEW CHRISTIANITY

Since World War II the Catholic Church has undergone major doctrinal shifts in response to fundamental changes in the world balance of power: the growth of the socialist camp from a single country into a community of independent states, and the development of national liberation struggles within the Third World. The Vatican has endeavored to make its peace with Marxism (*Pacem in Terris*) and then to break its established dependence on world capitalism or imperialism (*Populorum Progressio*). Besides this liberal position institutionalized by the Second Vatican Council (1962–5) and represented by the Christian Democratic parties in Latin America, the Church has also fathered radical and revolutionary currents in the form of a Christian New Left. These trends emerged not in the traditional Catholic centers of western Europe, but within the Third World and Latin America in particular.

The two most important leaders of this New Left in the 60s were Dom Helder Câmara, the radical Archbishop of Recife and Olinde, and the revolutionary priest Camilo Torres. In collaboration with seven other Brazilian bishops Helder Câmara took the initiative in formulating the 'Manifesto of Sixteen Bishops of the Third World' published in *Blackfriars* (London, December 1967), which justified social revolution and called upon the Church to condemn the capitalist system and to work with socialists in building a new social order. With other Brazilian bishops he pushed through the radical resolutions adopted at the Conference of Latin American Bishops (CELAM) at Medellín, Colombia, in August 1968, implicitly condemning US imperialism and justifying in principle armed insurrections against evident and prolonged oligarchical regimes in Latin America. In favoring a socialist revolution through peaceful and democratic means, Helder Câmara's Action for Justice and Peace, founded in 1968, was the ecclesiastical counterpart of Salvador Allende's Popular Unity coalition in Chile.

The revolutionary current within the Latin American Church was launched not by Helder Câmara, but by Camilo Torres. Several years before the radical stance formalized in the 'Manifesto of Sixteen Bishops of the Third World', Camilo inaugurated a movement among priests and laity in Colombia that began with roughly the same objectives, but ended with a positive commitment to Che's strategy of armed struggle (45). After joining the Guevarist-inspired Colombian ELN in December 1965, Camilo was killed in a military ambush on 15 February 1966. Camilo combined Christ's with Che's mandate to liberate men from human oppression: the duty of every Christian is to be a revolutionary, and the duty of every revolutionary is to make the revolution.

Other priests have followed his example, notably Father Juan Carlos Zaffaroni in Uruguay, who went underground in 1968 and was then accused of having joined the Tupamaros, and Father Domingo Laín, who returned to Colombia in 1970 to join the ELN after having been deported to his native Spain. Inspired by Camilo's example, by his articles and messages to the Colombian people, movements bearing his name soon appeared in other Latin American countries. In Colombia he inspired the Golconda Movement, in Venezuela the Camilo Torres Movement of the Christian Left, in Bolivia the NLF-Camilo Torres Brigade, in Chile the Camilo Torres Movement and the so-called Young Church, in Argentina the Camilo Torres Commandos and the Priests for the Third World – movements testifying to Camilo's direct influence but also to that of Che Guevara.

In Latin America the Catholic Church has traditionally been allied to the landed oligarchy. Its vitriolic censure of all shades of communism, socialism and even liberalism are well known. Yet more important to Camilism than the differences between official Catholic doctrine and revolutionary Marxism are the points of agreement between the Christian ethic and Che's concept of the new man. Each stresses the imperative of personal sacrifice and devotion to the cause of the wretched and oppressed. Among the various aspects of Che's legacy, his revolutionary ethic, heroic image and martyrdom have had the greatest impact on the Camilist tradition. At the same time, Camilists have also absorbed his revolutionary strategy. If Che's strategy of the insurrectionary foco finds acceptance in Catholic circles it is because the biblical tradition, from Moses to the Prophets, relied upon violence to secure God's will and the liberation of the Chosen People. For Camilists, the Chosen People today are the poor singled out by the New Testament beatitudes. Thus Camilo's followers stress the importance of the related themes of liberation and violence in the form of a new theology directly challenging the established one.

Camilism became a significant political force mainly through the efforts of the ex-seminarian Juan García Elorrio, whose bimonthly *Cristianismo y Revolución*, founded in Buenos Aires in 1966, began by diffusing Camilo's thought throughout the Southern Cone. From there he went on to found the Camilo Torres Commandos and the underground journal *Che Compañero*, under the direct influence of Guevarism and in resistance to the military dictatorship in Argentina. Juan García belonged to the Peronist Revolutionary Movement (MRP) and, with Cooke, represented the Argentine delegation at the OLAS Conference in Havana in August 1967. In February 1968 he organized the First Camilo Torres Latin American Encounter in Montevideo (46), attended by delegations from the Camilo Torres movements of Colombia, Chile, Uruguay and Argentina. Jailed in August 1969, he was mysteriously killed in a hit-and-run accident on 26 January 1970, a month after his release. The work of disseminating Camilism through the pages of *Cristianismo y Revolución* then fell to his companion and co-worker, Casiana Ahumada (47).

Politically, Camilism has had a disruptive effect on the Christian Democratic parties in Latin America. In Colombia the Social Christian Democratic Party supported Camilo's United Front against the oligarchy, until in September 1965 it withdrew in protest because of his pronouncements in favor of Cuba and support for armed actions against the government. This caused a split within its youth sector, several leading cadres and groups choosing to remain with Camilo. In Argentina the Christian Democratic Party was never able to build a significant constituency because of the rival Camilo Torres movement founded by García Elorrio. In Chile the Christian Democratic Party split in 1969 when its left wing founded a rival party, the United Movement for Popular Action (MAPU), which played a prominent role in Allende's government of Popular Unity. And in Bolivia the youth sector of the Christian Democratic Party split and founded the Revolutionary Christian Democracy (DCR), whose leading cadres joined the ELN in 1970, and afterwards collaborated in founding the Movement of the Revolutionary Left (MIR) in May 1971.

The role of Guevarism
in the industrially advanced countries

The insurrectional foco has been most effective against Latin American dictators, in Cuba from 1956 to 1959 and in Argentina from 1968 to 1973. It has also succeeded in its secondary aim of compelling oligarchical regimes to abandon their façade of constitutionality, notably in Brazil in 1968 and Uruguay in 1973. Except for Uruguay, these relative successes were achieved under the conditions originally spelled out by Che in *Guerrilla Warfare*: first, the existence of a government maintaining itself in power illegally; second, the impossibility of defending basic civil rights through constitutional or legal channels (*4*). Che took for granted that these conditions were in turn based on the syndrome of underdevelopment and superexploitation typical of dependent countries. The common denominator of all such countries he subsequently identified with the 'hunger of the people', their emptiness from being oppressed and exploited through low wages, underemployment, unemployment, and hunger in the literal sense. The objective conditions for applying the foco strategy were interpreted to include the popular expressions of that hunger, the resulting repression by the puppet governments and their sepoyan armies, and the escalation of social tensions generated by that repression (*5*).

Where these conditions are absent, as in the major powers of western Europe, in North America or in Japan, the three principal lessons of the Cuban Revolution cease to apply. In those countries a guerrilla force cannot develop into a people's army with the capacity of winning a war against the regular army; insurrectional focos are incapable of mobilizing the masses for revolution; and the principal terrain for waging an armed struggle must not be the countryside. A trial of strength is a caricature of Guevarism against a state strong and ready for battle, where legal channels permit a wide range of popular reforms and a margin for bargaining built on superprofits and the exploitation of people in the Third World. The mechanical transplantation of Che's strategy from the supporting conditions in the Third World to the conditions of comparative prosperity and political stability in the First World has yet to yield positive results for the simple reason that conditions there are as yet unsuited for armed confrontation.

In what respects, then, is Guevarism relevant to the advanced countries? Evidently, it is relevant to 'Third World' peoples within the First World, to national liberation struggles against internal colonialism. In the United States a Guevarist strategy was applied by the Blacks in their struggle for self-determination; in Canada it emerged in the movement for Quebec's independence; in the United Kingdom it aims at Irish unification. The Black Panther movement, the Quebec Liberation Front (FLQ) and the Irish Republican Army (IRA) each testifies in some degree to Guevarist influence. Although the Black Panthers were indebted mainly to Maoism, their leaders also paid tribute to the influence of Che and Debray. In an interview included in Nicholas Regush's *Pierre Vallières: The Revolutionary Process in Quebec* (New York, 1973), Vallières expressly acknowledged the importance of the Tupamaros and the armed movements in Argentina and Brazil in shaping the FLQ's strategy of urban guerrilla warfare. And in a 'Conversation with an Irish Militant' published in *Pensamiento Crítico* (Havana, June 1971), it is evident that the IRA also included a Guevarist tendency which, basing itself on Che's Algiers speech, identifies the Irish struggle for independence with that of Third World peoples generally.

The common denominator of all Guevarist movements in the advanced countries is the priority they assign to the international struggle against what they identify as imperialism and neo-imperialism. On the basis of Che's Algiers speech, they interpret every blow aimed by national liberation movements in the underdeveloped countries as a triumph for the exploited classes in the developed ones. For they see a direct link between class exploitation in the developed countries and neo-imperialist exploitation of whole nations in the Third World. On the premise that the superprofits from the exploitation of dependent countries constitute a major source of stability and support for capitalism in the economically independent ones, Guevarists in the advanced countries support every action aimed at weakening their common enemy.

Solidarity with Third World struggles is inseparably tied to another aspect of Guevarist movements in the First World: the strategy of confrontation or polarization of forces designed to challenge through direct action the economic, political and cultural hegemony of the capitalist class. Its rationale is taken from Che's 'Guerrilla Warfare: A Method', which aims at breaking down the liberal façade of superficially democratic regimes by obliging them to resort to violence and repressive legislation (5). Only through confrontation, Che argued, can governments be forced to a decision: to retreat before popular pressure or to call in the police and the regular army to quash popular demonstrations. The strategy of polarization is designed to upset the existing equilibrium of classes by forcing a showdown, by scrapping the traditional game of politics qua negotiation for a zero-sum game in which there are no winners without losers. This strategy is common not only to national liberation struggles, but also to student and worker movements within the First World. These movements, representing the interests of oppressed classes and strata of the dominant race or nationality, may be distinguished by their different forms of struggle: urban guerrilla warfare and extraparliamentary mass opposition.

URBAN GUERRILLA WARFARE

The first groups to adopt a Guevarist strategy of solidarity with Third World struggles were students and youth in the United States, followed by comparable movements in western Europe. Condemnation of the war in Vietnam and solidarity with the NLF was the crucial issue contributing to the formation of Guevarist action groups and the radicalization of the North American and German student organizations. Campus opposition focused on scientific research used to feed the US war machine. As the war escalated, student organizations gave birth to the first tiny urban guerrilla movements in the advanced countries: Weatherman in the US and the Red Army Fraction in West Germany.

The cadres of the Weatherman faction were initially formed on the campuses of the University of Michigan and Columbia University. In the fall of 1968 the University of Michigan chapter of Students for a Democratic Society (SDS) suffered a split between the 'Radical Caucus', in favor of student power and base-building, and the 'Jesse James Gang', advocating aggressive exposure of the imperialist and racist role of the university. Later, in March 1969, a roughly parallel split occurred in the Columbia chapter between the old leadership or 'Praxis-Axis' and Mark Rudd's 'Action-Faction'. The rebellion at Columbia University in April and May 1969, sparked and led by the 'Action-Faction', anticipated that the anti-War movement could be most effectively aided through the seizure of university buildings and the paralysis of the educational process rather than by talking to people or presenting a Marxist analysis. The split within SDS corresponded in Latin America to the 1965 split within the Peruvian MIR between the Guevarist advocates of a political-military confrontation (De la Puente) and the proponents of base-building (Napurí), who shortly withdrew from the MIR to organize Revolutionary Vanguard (VR).

Formally organized and elected to the leadership of SDS at its National Convention in Chicago in June 1969, Weatherman made evident its Guevarist proclivity from the beginning. It saw itself as a fifth column, operating behind enemy lines in support of the national liberation struggles of the NLF in Vietnam and of the Black Panthers in the US. Its political objective was undoubtedly Guevarist – the creation of strategic armed chaos aimed at the destruction of the imperialist state. At the Weatherman 'National War Council' held in

Flint, Michigan, in December 1969, an effort was made to adapt Debray's interpretation of the foco to guerrilla warfare in the United States (48). But the conditions for applying Guevarism in the US were not at all comparable to those in Latin America. Che always stressed that guerrilla warfare was to be a war of the masses, depending for its success on popular support. Weatherman never had such support.

The Red Army Fraction (RAF) emerged from promilitary cadres within the German Socialist Student Union (SDS). Unlike Weatherman, it represented only a small fraction of the membership of the revolutionary student movement. Neither did the RAF constitute a response to internal colonialism nor to a military draft for the war in Vietnam. Moreover, the RAF was a consequence rather than a cause of escalating repression against the German SDS. The shooting of Benno Ohnesorg in West Berlin on 2 June 1967, during a demonstration against the Shah of Iran, was followed by the shooting of Rudi Dutschke, the leader of SDS, in April 1968. The mass mobilizations of students against the Vietnam War were met by police brutality that exceeded anything comparable in other west European countries. This was evident before the RAF formally emerged as an urban guerrilla movement in August 1970.

In May 1970 Andreas Baader escaped from a term in prison through the armed intervention of Ulrike Meinhof. Members of his group then traveled via East Berlin to Jordan, where they received military training from Al Fatah. After their return in August, they attacked three West Berlin banks within a few minutes of each other. Over the next two years the expropriated funds were used to build the logistical infrastructure of the RAF and to train military cadres. Apartments and houses were obtained in various places in West Germany, along with automobiles, weapons and explosives. On 11 May 1972 the first exemplary attack occurred with the bombing of the officers' club at the headquarters of the American army in Frankfurt. This was followed by the bombing of police headquarters in Augsburg and Munich. The right-wing Axel Springer publishing house in Hamburg was bombed on 19 May, after which the RAF attacked the headquarters of the American army in Heidelberg on 24 May.

Like Weatherman, the 'Baader-Meinhof Gang', as it was referred to in the press, made a fetish of bombings and became identified with acts of destruction' that were only indirectly related to the basic struggles of the working class (49). In Uruguay and Argentina the abductions of managers and company executives were aimed at the immediate enemies of the people; they helped to get across-the-board wage increases and to settle other grievances and strikes on terms favorable to the workers. From the beginning, the Tupamaros and most of the Argentine guerrillas had deep roots in the labor movement. By contrast, the RAF did not have any corresponding links with the German workers, nor was it successful in recruiting their support. Although it gave more attention than Weatherman to building a logistical infrastructure, its commencement of armed struggle was no less premature.

EXTRAPARLIAMENTARY MASS OPPOSITION

During the May 1968 revolt in France, Guevarism made its deepest impression yet on the student movement, in the March 22nd Movement, the Revolutionary Communist Youth (JCR), the National Vietnam Committee (CVN), and the Committees of Initiative for a Revolutionary Youth Front. Unlike Weatherman and the RAF, the French followers of Guevara concentrated on mass demonstrations without simultaneous military preparations. The outcome of this strategy was that when conditions became ripe for armed struggle, it was too late to prepare for one.

Basically, this was the mistake of the Guevarist currents in France from November 1967 to June 1968. The first principle of the March 22nd Movement was that revolutionary unity be achieved directly through action rather than political debate. This principle was supported by another, that each organization renounce its claim to be the sole representative of the vanguard, as if only *its* political line were the 'correct' one. Both principles were underscored by the overtly Guevarist Committees of Initiative for a Revolutionary Youth Front. However, when the Pompidou government dissolved it and other like organizations by decree on 12 June 1968, they were unprepared to go underground or to continue the struggle through extralegal means.

Only in Italy, where the Communist Party is comparatively stronger than in any other west European country, did Guevarism reach below the level of student protest to penetrate the left wing of the labor movement. Since emerging in Italy in the 60s, *Lotta Continua* has been the most promising and novel Guevarist organization for direct mass action in western Europe. Like other Guevarist organizations, it maintains direct contact with corresponding movements of liberation in the Third World, notably with Douglas Bravo's FALN in Venezuela. But, unlike most of them, it is an organization of workers rather than of students or revolutionary intellectuals.

The task of the revolutionary vanguard, for *Lotta Continua*, is to prepare the workers for armed actions through utilizing all the possibilities of legal struggle. These include not only strikes for higher wages and improved conditions of work, but above all the development of an extraparliamentary and extra-trade-union opposition operating independently of the established parties and trade-union bureaucracies. In the organization of wildcat strikes, slowdowns and impromptu political demonstrations, *Lotta Continua* has not hesitated to resort to illegal actions, but is opposed to armed confrontations until the objective conditions have matured.

Unlike *Il Manifesto* and *Potere Operaio*, its extraparliamentary rivals on the left, *Lotta Continua* has gone beyond Maoism to the assimilation of the lessons of Guevarism for western Europe. Its principal objective is the overcoming of US imperialism through the internationalization of the class struggle – a struggle tied to the costs of the Vietnam War unloaded upon the workers of western Europe. In an analysis of the international situation in its fall 1970 issue of *Comunismo* (Milan), *Lotta Continua* showed how escalating war expenditures by the US had led to an unfavorable balance of trade with western Europe, tantamount to an overall increase in the demand for European commodities without a corresponding increase in the supply of American goods. Far from prejudicial to the interests of European capitalists, this dumping of the burden of US inflation on the European economies had been more than compensated by an accumulation of reserves of US dollars from their expanding exports to the US. The outcome of this complex mechanism of international trade linked to the war in Vietnam is that North American and European workers have had to pay the costs of that war through a subtle attack on their standard of living. In this perspective, the interests of west European capital appear tied to those of US imperialism in Vietnam, while the interests of west European workers appear correspondingly tied to the struggle against US imperialism on an international scale.

In response to the erosion in their standard of living, west European workers began showing signs of increased militancy during and following the May 1968 student uprising in France. This recovery of militancy was met by an increase in repressive legislation throughout Europe, by the emergency laws in Germany and the laws of public security in Italy. Against this new wave of political repression, *Lotta Continua* advocates direct mass opposition to the bourgeois state and its norms of labor discipline and productivity – a struggle aimed at hitting the capitalists where it hurts most (*50*). Its goal is to paralyze the economic system through waves of wildcat strikes, slowdowns and other forms of industrial sabotage, combined with the refusal to accept a political settlement at the polls. In effect, *Lotta Continua* favors a displacement of the Weatherman strategy from the streets to the factories and other centers of production.

In view of its applications to advanced as well as underdeveloped countries, Guevarism represents a mode of oppositional politics designed to replace that of the established Communist parties. But it can hardly compare in strength and importance to them. In the advanced countries, where the symbolic aspect of Che's legacy is the rule rather than the exception, Guevarism has yet to become a significant or influential movement. In underdeveloped Latin America, where the political and strategic aspects of his legacy prevail over the symbolic, it is still little more than a side-current of the main line and drift of the Cuban Revolution. Nonetheless, Guevarism has contributed to a reawakening of Leninist currents within the traditional CP's and, by focusing attention on the strategy and tactics of armed struggle, has indirectly contributed to a more versatile action program combining all forms of resistance to military and legal oppression.

Although its principal limitation is to have degenerated into the politics of rival sects and splinter groups, especially in the advanced countries, in the Southern Cone of Latin America it has approached the status of a mass movement through its influence on the Tupamaros, the Chilean MIR and the Argentine ERP. Perhaps its greatest success to date is to have acquired a foothold in the Peronist Movement through the unified FAR-Montoneros and their political arm, the Peronist Youth. While Guevarists elsewhere continue to overrate the role of a political-military vanguard, in Argentina they insist that there can be no revolutionary leadership without a mass following. Thus the Argentine FAR has initiated a new phase in the development of Guevarism by integrating the insurrectional foco with the politics of a mass organization. In the decades to come, this tendency promises to become the most enduring aspect of Che's legacy.

Part One
The Development of Guevarism

a IMPACT OF THE CUBAN REVOLUTION

The Cuban guerrilla experience contributed to the development of Guevarism in two significant respects: it was the principal source of Che's reflections on revolutionary strategy, on the difficulties associated with starting a revolution and leading one to victory; and it became the basis of his theory of the origins of revolution and of how and why the guerrillas were able to triumph over a superior military force.

The strategy for the overthrow of Batista first propounded by Che in El Cubano Libre, the monthly mimeographed organ founded by him in late October 1957, called for the sabotage of sugar production by the peasants and the launching of a political general strike by organized labor. This strategy, which took the role of organized labor to be decisive, was later abandoned in view of the lessons of the abortive general strike of 9 April 1958. The germs of the foco strategy were contained in these lessons of the April strike.

The theoretical problems associated with the Cuban Revolution had to wait until the insurrectionary phase was over for Che to treat them systematically. His most important contribution to an understanding of the origins of the Revolution was his April 1961 essay, which examines the objective and subjective conditions necessary for the emergence of a revolutionary situation and the launching of an armed struggle. His explanation of the political development of the guerrillas and their successful response to the problems involved in fighting the regular army is central to his October 1960 study of the ideology of the Revolution.

1 Mobilization of the Masses: Systematic Sabotage of Sugar Production and the Organization of a General Strike *CHE GUEVARA*

The Sierra Maestra is approaching the end of its historic role as the impregnable bastion against the mercenary army and is preparing to launch its load of combatants upon the plains.

Victory on the plains will be supported by two great weapons of the people: the systematic burning of the cane fields that will undermine the economic roots of the regime; and the revolutionary general strike which will mean the final blow and the triumph over the repressive forces.

It is unnecessary to point out the vital importance of the burning of the sugar-cane, which provides the taxes for supporting the regime's enormous repressive apparatus.

Undoubtedly, there will be those who, on the basis of false humanitarian scruples or the damage to the country's economic structure, will reject these measures. To them we respond: we cannot burn the cane on all the island through the actions of a hot-headed group; for that, we need the active collaboration of the people. If the working masses do not follow our slogan, there will be no large-scale burning of the cane. We must face the challenge. Either we must give good reasons for burning all the cane or be shown the contrary through the failure to burn it. We have faith in the people's judgment. The revolutionary general strike is the decisive weapon, the intercontinental projectile of the peoples. There is no repressive organization capable of defeating it when carried through to the end with discipline and enthusiasm.

In the future it will be our unquestioned duty to organize the general strike down to the last detail. We must show how the interests of distinct classes are served by the great revolutionary truth: there is nothing worse than Batista; united, we shall prevail. Pickets must be organized to paralyze every intent to break the strike; sabotage teams, to destroy completely the enemy's lines of communication. Each person must become aware that the next general strike will not be a spontaneous and limited one, but will be organized, general and revolutionary. That will be our victory.

Che Guevara, 'Editorial', *El Cubano Libre* (Sierra Maestra), No. 1, November 1957, abridged.

2 There Can Be No Revolutionary Movement without a Correct Assessment of Historical Reality
CHE GUEVARA

This is a singular revolution in which some have thought to find a disagreement with one of the most orthodox premises of the revolutionary movement, that expressed by Lenin: 'without a revolutionary theory, there can be no revolutionary movement'. It would be more suitable to say that revolutionary theory, as an expression of social reality, is more important than any dictum. That is, even without knowing theory, a revolution may be made if one interprets correctly historical reality and if one uses correctly the forces available. It is clear that a knowledge of theory simplifies the task and prevents us from falling into dangerous errors, as long as that theory corresponds to reality. Moreover, speaking concretely of our revolution, we must reiterate that its principal actors were not exactly theoreticians, although neither were they ignorant of the major social phenomena and the laws governing them. This made it possible, on the basis of some theoretical knowledge and the profound knowledge of reality, to develop a revolutionary theory.

The foregoing must be considered a prologue to the explanation of this curious phenomenon which has intrigued the whole world: the Cuban Revolution. How and why a group of men, cut to pieces by an army enormously superior in technique and equipment, succeeded first in surviving, then in making itself strong and eventually stronger than the enemy in the battle-zones, later in emigrating toward new battle-fronts in order finally to defeat the enemy in pitched battles – yet with troops very inferior in numbers – is a feat worthy of study in the history of the contemporary world.

79

Naturally, we, who do not often show a due respect for theory, have not come today to expound, as its owners, the reality of the Cuban Revolution: we simply want to discuss the bases for interpreting that reality. In fact, it is necessary to separate the Cuban Revolution into two absolutely different stages: that of armed action until 1 January 1959; and, after that, the stage of political, economic and social transformation.

Even these two stages require successive subdivisions, although we shall not interpret them from the point of view of historical exposition, but rather from the perspective of the evolution of the revolutionary thought of the leaders through their contact with the people. . . .

Before the landing of the *Granma*, a mentality prevailed that up to a certain point could be called subjectivist: the blind confidence in a rapid popular explosion; the enthusiasm and faith in a quick uprising combined with spontaneous revolutionary strikes and the subsequent fall of the dictator. . . .

After the landing came the defeat, the almost total destruction of the group and its reorganization in the form of guerrillas. Already, the small number of survivors – moreover, survivors with a will to struggle – had come to understand the falsity of the imagined scheme of spontaneous uprisings throughout the island, and to realize that the struggle would have to be a long one and would have to rely upon extensive peasant participation. . . . During this stage two things became evident, both very important for the groups involved: for the peasants, that the army's persecutions and brutalities were not enough to finish off the guerrillas, but did suffice to destroy their houses, their harvests and their families, for which a good solution was to take refuge with the guerrillas where their lives would be safe; for the guerrillas, that it was increasingly necessary to win over the peasant masses, to whom they obviously had to offer something the peasants longed for with all their might. . . .

The successes of our rebel forces began filtering through the censorship and the people were rapidly approaching the climax of their revolutionary activity. It was then that from Havana came the plan for a revolutionary general strike throughout the national territory that should destroy the force of the enemy, attacking it everywhere at once. The function of the Rebel Army would, in this case, be that of a catalyst or, perhaps, that of an 'irritating thorn' for unleashing the movement. . . .

The revolutionary strike, however, was not adequately prepared, since it disregarded the importance of labor unity and did not look to the workers, in the course of their own revolutionary activity, to choose the right moment. Its organizers tried to launch a clandestine coup, calling the strike from a radio, not knowing that the secret of the day and the hour had filtered through to the authorities, but not to the people. The strike movement collapsed, while a select number of revolutionary patriots were mercilessly assassinated. . . .

In this moment one of the most important qualitative changes occurred in the development of the revolutionary war: the certainty that victory would be achieved only through the growth of the guerrilla forces, until the defeat of the enemy army in pitched battles.

Che Guevara, 'Notas para el estudio de la ideología de
la Revolución Cubana' (October 1960), *Obras*
1957–1967 (Havana, 1970), Vol. II, pp. 92–3, 95, 96, 98,
abridged.

3 Hunger of the People: The Conditions for Starting a Revolution   CHE GUEVARA

We, the peoples of America, are called by another suave and shamefaced name: 'underdeveloped'.

What is underdevelopment?

A dwarf with an enormous head and swollen chest is 'underdeveloped', inasmuch as his weak legs and short arms fail to correspond with the rest of his anatomy; he is the product of a pathological phenomenon that has distorted his development. That is what we actually are, the gently-termed 'underdeveloped' countries, in reality colonial, semicolonial or dependent ones. We are countries with economies distorted by imperialism, countries which have abnormally developed the industrial or agricultural branches necessary to complement its complex economy. 'Underdevelopment' or distorted development carries with it dangerous specifications in primary goods, which threaten with hunger all our peoples. We, the 'underdeveloped', are also countries of a single product and a single market – a single product whose uncertain sales depend on a single market which imposes and fixes the terms of trade. Here we have the great formula of imperialist economic domination, added to the old yet eternally young Roman motto of 'divide and conquer'.

The great landed properties, then, through their connections with imperialism, completely shape the so-called 'underdevelopment' which has for its result low wages and unemployment. This phenomenon of low wages and unemployment gives rise to a vicious cycle that results in ever lower wages and ever greater unemployment, as the great contradictions of the system become more acute and, constantly at the mercy of cyclical variations in the economy, create the common denominator of the peoples of America from the Rio Grande to the South Pole. That common denominator, which we write in capitals and which serves as the basis of analysis for all those who reflect upon these social phenomena, is called the HUNGER OF THE PEOPLE: exhaustion from being oppressed, harassed, exploited to the maximum, exhaustion from selling daily one's miserable labor-power from fear of joining the enormous mass of unemployed – in order that from each human body the maximum profits may be squeezed, afterwards to be squandered in the orgies of the owners of capital. . . .

All this existed in Cuba. Here too we had hunger; here there was one of the highest rates of unemployment in Latin America; here imperialism was more ruthless than in many of the countries of America; and here the great landed properties existed with as much force as in any brother country.

What did we do to liberate ourselves from this great phenomenon of imperialism with its sequel of puppet governments in each country and mercenary armies, disposed to defend each puppet and the entire complex social system of the exploitation of man by man? Let us apply some formulas which we have already given as a discovery of our empirical medicine for the great ills of our beloved Latin America, an empirical medicine that is now scientifically confirmed.

The objective conditions for the struggle are given by the hunger of the people, the immediate response to that hunger, the fear generated in order to put off a popular explosion, and the wave of loathing that repression creates. Missing in America are the subjective conditions of which the most important is the awareness of the possibility of victory over the imperial powers and their internal allies by taking the violent road. Those conditions are created by means of the armed struggle which helps to anticipate and clarify the inevitability of change, the inevitability of the defeat of the army by the popular forces and of its subsequent annihilation, as a necessary condition of every authentic revolution.

Che Guevara, 'Cuba: excepción histórica o vanguardia
en la lucha anticolonialista?' (April 1961), *Obras*
1957–1967 (Havana, 1970), Vol. II, pp. 409–10, 410–11,
abridged.

b EVOLUTION OF THE FOCO STRATEGY

The immediate problem of the insurrectionary phase of the Cuban Revolution was how to launch an armed movement and then to survive against the forces of repression. This required a new type of organization, the guerrilla foco or nucleus, and a corresponding strategy that was developed by Che only after the insurrectionary phase was over in Cuba, if not in the rest of Latin America. Thus the evolution of the foco strategy was posterior to the events of the Cuban Revolution. As the choice of documents indicates, the foco strategy evolved through three principal stages. The first limited the viability of armed struggles to those against unconstitutional governments and Latin American dictators. The second extended those limits to include military operations against pseudo-democratic regimes whose populism was mainly verbal. The third included within the scope of such operations a direct confrontation with US imperialism, identified as the principal bulwark of reformist governments as well as of reactionary military regimes in Latin America.

4 The Armed Vanguard in the Struggle against Caribbean-Type Dictatorships   CHE GUEVARA

We consider that the Cuban Revolution made three fundamental contributions to the mechanics of revolutionary movements in America:

(1) The popular forces can win a war against the army.
(2) It is not always necessary to wait for all the conditions of revolution to be given; the insurrectionary foco can create them.
(3) In underdeveloped America the terrain for armed struggle should be basically in the countryside.

Of these three contributions, the first two are directed against the passive attitude of revolutionaries or pseudo-revolutionaries, who seek support for their inactivity in the pretext that nothing can be done against a professional army, who sit down to wait for all the necessary objective and subjective conditions to be mechanically given without attempting to accelerate them. As the world knows, these two contributions were formerly a subject of discussion in Cuba and are probably still discussed in America.

Naturally, when one talks about the conditions of revolution, one should not think that all of them can be created through the impulse given to them by the guerrilla foco. One must always consider that there is a minimum of conditions necessary to the establishment and consolidation of the first foco. That is, it is necessary to show the people the impossibility of defending their social rights within the framework of peaceful struggle. Inevitably, the peace is broken by the oppressive forces which maintain themselves in power in violation of established law.

In these conditions popular discontent begins to take increasingly assertive forms; a disposition to resistance crystallizes in a given moment in an outbreak of fighting, provoked initially by the attitude of the authorities.

When a government has risen to power through some form of popular consent, fraudulent or not, and maintains at least a semblance of constitutional legality, the development of guerrillas cannot be promoted because the possibilities of peaceful struggle have not been exhausted.

The third contribution is fundamentally strategic in character and should be noted by those who would base dogmatically the mass struggle on movements in the cities, completely forgetting the immense participation of people in the countryside in the life of all the underdeveloped countries of America. One should not underestimate the struggles of organized workers, but should analyze realistically the possibilities, in the difficult conditions of armed struggle, where the guarantees that customarily adorn our constitutions are suspended or ignored. In these conditions the workers' movements confront enormous dangers: they must operate outside the law, clandestinely and without arms. The situation in the countryside is not as difficult, where the inhabitants are supported by the armed guerrillas and in places where the repressive forces cannot reach. . . .

When we analyze in depth the war tactics of the guerrillas, we see that the guerrilla must have an exact knowledge of the terrain in which he operates, the paths of access and retreat, the possibilities of rapid maneuver, the extent of popular support, naturally, and hiding places. All this indicates that the guerrilla will engage in actions in rural and barely populated places and that the people's struggle for their rights will be focused preferably and almost exclusively on changing the social form of land ownership. That is, the guerrilla is above all an agrarian reformer. He interprets the desires of the great mass of peasants who want to own the land they cultivate, the means of production, the animals, and everything they have longed for over the years that constitutes their life and will also constitute their cemetery.

Che Guevara, 'La guerra de guerrillas' (1960), *Obras 1957–1967* (Havana, 1970), Vol. I, pp. 31–2, 34, abridged.

5 The Generalization of the Foco to Cover the Struggle against Pseudo-Democracies and the National Bourgeoisie *CHE GUEVARA*

We see today in Latin America a state of unstable equilibrium between oligarchical dictatorship and popular pressure. The word 'oligarchical' is used to define the reactionary alliance between the bourgeoisie and the landlord class of each country with a greater or lesser preponderance of feudal structures. These dictatorships exist within a certain margin of legality established to serve their own ends during the period of unrestricted class domination; but we are now passing through an epoch in which popular demands are growing in intensity. The masses are knocking on the doors of bourgeois legality, which in turn will be violated by its own authors in order to stifle the will of the masses. The problem for the ruling classes is that open violations, contrary to already established legislation – or even to retrospective legislation designed to sanctify the deed – further antagonize the popular forces. Thus the oligarchical dictatorship tries to use the old legal means to change the constitution and depress further the proletariat without encouraging a direct confrontation. Nevertheless, the confrontation is still produced. The people can no longer bear the old and, even less, the new coercive measures established by the dictatorship, and will attempt to violate them. We should never forget the classist, authoritarian and restrictive nature of the bourgeois state. . . .

We must not allow, in other words, that the word 'democracy', utilized in apologetic fashion to designate the dictatorship of the exploiting classes, should lose its profound significance and come to mean only certain liberties granted to the citizen. To fight solely for the restoration of bourgeois legality without posing the question of revolutionary power is to struggle for a return to a dictatorial order pre-established by the dominant social classes. That would be a struggle for lighter chains on the prisoner.

In conditions of conflict the oligarchy breaks its own contracts, destroys its own superficial 'democracy' and attacks the people, although it will also use methods of the superstructure created for oppression. At this moment the dilemma arises again: What should we do? Our answer is that violence is not the exclusive property of the exploiters, that the exploited can and should use it at the proper time. . . .

The national bourgeoisies have, in the majority, banded together with US imperialism, and their fate should be the same as that of imperialism in every country. Even when pacts are drawn between the national bourgeoisies and other imperialist powers or when either of these develops a coincidental contradiction with US imperialism, this occurs within the boundaries of a more fundamental struggle which, in the course of its development, will necessarily bring into conflict *all the exploited* and *all the exploiters*. This polarization of classes into opposing forces has so far been more rapid than the development of contradictions among exploiters over the division of the spoils. There are two sides: the alternative becomes increasingly clear for every individual and for each sector of the population.

Che Guevara, 'Guerra de guerrillas: Un método'
(September 1963), *Obras 1957–1967* (Havana, 1970),
Vol. I, pp. 165–6, 178, abridged.

6 The Internationalization of the Revolution: The Road to Vietnam *CHE GUEVARA*

Latin America forms a more or less homogeneous grouping, and in virtually all of its territory US monopoly capital maintains absolute control. The puppet governments or, in the best of cases, the weak or fearful ones cannot disobey orders from their Yankee boss. The North Americans have almost reached their maximum level of political and economic domination and cannot advance much further; thus any change in the situation could become a step backward for their hegemony. Their policy is to hold on to what they have already conquered. Their present course of action is reduced to the use of brute force to stop liberation movements of any kind.

Under the slogan 'We will not allow another Cuba' is hidden the possibility of treacherous aggressions, like that perpetrated against Santo Domingo or, earlier, the massacre in Panama, and the direct warning that Yankee troops are prepared to intervene anywhere in Latin America where the established order and US interests are threatened. This policy can be conducted with an almost absolute impunity. The OAS, however discredited it may be, is a convenient mask; the UN's inefficiency is both ridiculous and tragic; the armies of all Latin American countries are ready to intervene in order to crush their people. The International of Crime and Treason has indeed been established.

The indigenous bourgeoisies have lost all capacity to oppose imperialism – if you concede that they ever had any – and they are only appendages of imperialism. There are no more 'changes' to be made; the choice is socialist revolution or a caricature of revolution. . . .

New wars will erupt in several American countries, as has already happened in Bolivia, and they will intensify despite the perils inherent in the tasks of the modern revolutionary. Many will die as victims of their own errors, others will fall in the harsh combat that approaches; new fighters and leaders will be forged in the fire of revolutionary struggle. The people will choose their warriors and their leaders within the selective limits of the war itself; and the number of Yankee agents of oppression will increase. Today there are US advisors in all countries where there is armed struggle; and the Peruvian army, advised and trained by the Yankees, apparently won a battle with the revolutionaries of that country. But if the guerrilla focos operate with sufficient political and military dexterity, they will become virtually invincible and thereby force new interventions from the Yankees. Even in Peru new people, not yet well known, are tenaciously reorganizing the guerrilla struggle. The obsolete weapons which suffice to repress the small armed groups will gradually be replaced by modern weapons, as will the group of advisors by US soldiers. Then, the US will reach a point at which it is compelled to send increasing numbers of regular troops in an attempt to insure the relative stability of a nation whose national puppet army is collapsing before the guerrilla battles. This is the road to Vietnam; it is the path that the people should follow; it is the course that America will take. Its distinctive characteristic is that the armed groups should establish something similar to Juntas of Co-ordination in order to make the repressive tasks of Yankee imperialism more difficult and to facilitate our own cause.

Latin America, the continent ignored by recent liberation struggles, which begins to make its voice heard with the Tricontinental as the vanguard of the people, will have an extraordinary mission: the creation of the second or third Vietnam – or of the second and third Vietnams [in this part] of the world.

We must always remember that imperialism, the final stage of capitalism, is an international system, and we must fight it on a global scale. The strategic objective of this struggle is the destruction of imperialism.

Che Guevara, 'Mensaje a los pueblos del mundo a través de la Tricontinental' (April 1967), *Obras 1957–1967* (Havana, 1970), Vol. II, pp. 588–9, 593–4, abridged.

c THE POSTINSURRECTIONARY PHASE

During the postinsurrectionary phase of the Cuban Revolution beginning with the seizure of power on 1 January 1959, Che became involved with the practical tasks of overcoming Cuba's political and economic dependence on the US. In response to US efforts to sabotage the nationalization of basic industries on the island, followed by the US-supported Bay of Pigs invasion in April 1961, Che turned his attention to the institutional means of building a new socialist order as the indispensable condition of Cuba's political and economic independence. To build a new socialist society, he argued, one had to begin by creating a Marxist–Leninist vanguard party. As the first document indicates, this party was to have two fundamental goals: the development of production and the creation of revolutionary consciousness. The second document contains Che's specific economic strategy for transforming Cuba into an economically independent country, while the third discusses the objective conditions required to shape the new man and the subjective conditions or qualities of character required to build a new society.

7 Fundamental Tasks of the Vanguard Party
CHE GUEVARA

As the task of building socialism is confronted, we should avoid mechanical thinking as if it were the plague. Mechanical thinking leads only to stereotyped forms, secret cliques, favoritism and a host of evils within the revolutionary organization. It is necessary to work dialectically, gaining support from the masses, being always in contact with the masses, leading them by their example, using Marxist ideology and dialectical materialism, and being creative at all times.

What are the most important tasks for a member of the United Revolutionary Party? There are two fundamental ones, which constantly recur and which form the basis for all social development: production or the creation of goods for the people and the deepening of revolutionary consciousness.

I don't believe it necessary to explain to you the importance of production. A Party member should always be concerned with production.

Socialism is not a benevolent society; it is not a Utopian regime based on good will toward man. Socialism is a society that is reached through history, which has as its basis the socialization of the fundamental means of production and the equitable distribution of all social wealth, all within the context of social production. These means of production were created by capitalism: the large factories, the huge capitalist farms, the workshops where work is performed in association; but in that epoch the profits from the workers' labor were taken by the capitalists, by the exploiting class, by the legal owners of the means of production.

Things have changed now, but the basis is the same: a social class, a social structure that is necessarily built upon the previous one. And the process of building socialism is the development of all of our production.

And why consciousness? Consciousness is even more important, if that is possible. It is important because of the new characteristics of social development in this century.

When Marx made his analysis of societies, those known to have existed were a primitive society, a slave society, a feudal society, and finally a capitalist society. What Marx did was to analyze the basis for each. He showed that everything was related to production, that man's consciousness was determined by the environment in which he lived and that the environment was created by the relationships of production.

In sharpening the analysis, Marx did something even more important; he demonstrated that, historically, capitalism was to disappear and be replaced by a new society: socialism.

With the passing of time, Lenin further developed the analysis and reached the conclusion that the transition from one society to another was not a mechanical step, but rather that conditions could be accelerated to the maximum by means of what we might call 'catalysts' (that is my term, not Lenin's, but the idea is the same). In other words, given a vanguard of the proletariat capable of representing the workers' interests, with a clear idea of where it wished to go – to attempt to take power in order to establish the new society – then it would be possible to leap over stages. He furthermore believed that socialism could be developed in a single isolated country, even under the terrible conditions imposed by an imperialist encirclement, which is what the Soviet Union had to confront during the first years of the creation of its state. Thus, one begins to understand why consciousness is so important.

Che Guevara, 'Sobre la construcción del Partido'
(March 1963), *Obras 1957–1967* (Havana, 1970), Vol. II,
pp. 191–2, abridged.

8 The Budgetary System of Finance   CHE GUEVARA

Between the self-management system (cost-accounting system) and the budgetary system of finance there are differences of varying degrees. Our intention is to divide these differences into two broad categories and to explain them in general terms. There are differences in methodology and differences in substance, which must be explained carefully in order that this analysis shall not appear Byzantine.

It should be clearly stated now that what we are seeking is a more efficient way to reach communism. There are no differences in principle. The self-management system has demonstrated its practical efficiency; and, with a point of departure in identical bases, the same objectives are also posed. We believe that the plan of action for our system, if properly developed, can increase the economic efficiency of the socialist state, strengthen mass consciousness, and make the international socialist system more cohesive with a basis in united action.

The most obvious difference arises when we speak of the enterprise. The enterprise is for us a grouping of factories and units which have a similar technological base, a common objective in production or, in some cases, a restricted geographical area. In the self-management system an enterprise is a unit of production with its own legal status. A sugar mill is for the self-management system an enterprise, while for us all of the sugar refineries and other groupings related to sugar constitute the Consolidated Sugar Enterprise. . . .

Another difference is in the manner of using money. In our system it only functions as 'arithmetical money', as a reflection in prices of the progress of the enterprise, which the central organs are to analyze for the purpose of exercising proper control of its operations. For the self-management system, money not only has this role but is also used as a means of funding that acts as an indirect instrument of control. These funds allow the unit to operate; and its relation to the bank or source of funding is similar to that of a private enterprise in contact with capitalist banks, to which it must constantly explain its plans and demonstrate its solvency.

Naturally, in the case of the self-management system decisions are not made on a purely arbitrary basis; they conform to a plan and are co-ordinated among organizations of the state.

It follows that with respect to the utilization of money, our enterprises do not have their own funds. In the bank there are separate accounts for withdrawals and deposits. The enterprise withdraws funds according to the plan: from the general account for expenses and from the special account for salaries. However, deposits made by the enterprise are automatically transferred to the state.

The enterprises in the majority of our fellow socialist countries have their own funds in the banks, backed by bank credits and earning interest. It should never be forgotten that both the funds of the enterprises and the credits belong to society, and that the movement of the funds expresses the financial state of the enterprise.

With respect to work standards, the enterprises under self-management rely on time-schedules required to complete an assignment [presumably on the basis of time-studies], and work by the hour or by the piece. We are trying to convert all of our factories to using time-schedules, with bonuses for overproduction limited by the scale for maximum rate of pay. . . .

While reiterating that under both systems the general plan of the state is the maximum authority and that it must be respected, let us synthesize the operational differences between the two. Decentralizing tendencies are more pronounced in the self-management system, which exercises indirect control by means of the ruble or the bank, and the monetary results of the enterprise's activities serve as rewards. Material interest is the great lever that moves workers individually and collectively.

The budgetary system of financing, on the other hand, is based on centralized control of the enterprise's activities. Its plan and its economic functioning are controlled by central organs in a direct way. The enterprise has no funds of its own, nor does it receive bank credits. It utilizes, in an individual sense, material incentives, i.e., individual monetary rewards and punishments. At the proper time this system will also use collective incentives, but direct material reward is limited by the salary schedule.

Che Guevara, 'Sobre el sistema presupuestario de financiamiento' (February 1964), *Obras 1957–1967* (Havana, 1970), Vol. II, pp. 260–3, abridged.

9 The Creation of the New Man   CHE GUEVARA

The new society being created must compete harshly with the past. This is felt not only in the individual conscience, still residually influenced by an educational system systematically oriented toward the isolation of the individual, but also by the very character of this period of transition, marked by the persistence of business relationships. The commodity is the economic cell of capitalist society. As long as it exists, its effects will be felt in the organization of production and thus in consciousness.

Marx conceived of the period of transition as a result of the explosive transformation of the capitalist system, destroyed by its contradictions. Lenin later observed that some countries – the weak branches – were to fall from the tree of imperialism. In these countries capitalism has developed sufficiently to make its effects felt in one way or another on the people; but its own internal contradictions are not powerful enough to destroy the system. A liberation struggle against an external oppressor, suffering caused by foreign events, such as war, which drives the privileged classes against the exploited, and liberation movements directed against neocolonialist regimes, are among the common causes which break off the weaker links. Conscious action does the rest.

In these countries there is no form of education for worthwhile social labor, and wealth remains distant from the masses. Underdevelopment, on one hand, and the habitual flow of capital toward 'civilized' countries, on the other, make it impossible to change rapidly without sacrifice. There remains a long road to be traversed in order to construct a solid economic base; and the temptation to follow the paths of material interest, used as a stimulus for accelerated development, is very great.

One runs the risk of not seeing the forest for the trees. In chasing the chimera of achieving socialism with the rusty arms inherited from capitalism (the commodity as the economic unit, rate of profit, individual material interest as a lever, etc.), one may end up on a dead-end road. And you get there after traveling a long distance, criss-crossed by so many paths that it is difficult to remember when you took the wrong road. In the meantime, the economic basis chosen has eroded the development of consciousness. . . .

Allow me to say, at the risk of seeming ridiculous, that the true revolutionary is guided by great feelings of love. It is impossible to imagine an authentic revolutionary without this quality. Perhaps this is one of the great dramas of the leader. He must unite a passionate spirit with a cool mind and must make painful decisions without flinching. Our revolutionaries of the vanguard have to idealize that love for the people, for the most sacred causes, and make it one and indivisible. They cannot merely descend with a small, daily dose of kindness to the places where the common man practices kindness on a broader scale.

The leaders of the revolution have children who, in their first words, do not say their father's name; wives who must sacrifice part of their lives in order to bring the revolution to fruition. The circle of friendship is restricted to companions of the revolution. There is no life apart from it.

Under these conditions, one must have a feeling for humanity, a feeling for justice and truth in order not to fall into dogmatic extremes, cold scholasticism, and isolation from the masses. It is necessary to struggle every day so that the love for living humanity may be transformed into concrete deeds, into actions that may serve as examples and inspiration.

The revolutionary, ideological motor of the revolution within his party, consumes himself in a ceaseless activity which has no end except death, unless socialist construction is achieved on a worldwide level. If his revolutionary spirit lessens when the most rewarding tasks are accomplished on a local level, and proletarian internationalism is forgotten, the revolution he leads will cease to be a dynamic force. It will fall into a comfortable slumber and become easy prey for our irreconcilable enemies. Imperialism will take the lead. Proletarian internationalism is a duty and it is also a revolutionary necessity. Thus do we teach our people.

Che Guevara, 'El socialismo y el hombre en Cuba'
(March 1965), *Obras 1957–1967* (Havana, 1970), Vol. II,
pp. 371–2, 382, abridged.

Part Two
Divisions within Guevarism

a VANGUARDIST VERSUS MILITARIST TENDENCIES

During the 60s and early 70s Guevarist debates over the comparative merits of vanguardist and militarist tendencies took two principal forms. First, there was the irresolvable opposition between the extreme partisans of each as represented by the Salvadoran CP ('The party has no use for a foco at this stage of the struggle') and the Bolivian ELN ('The foco has no need of a party at this stage of the struggle'). Second, there were the differences in starting-point represented by the Peruvian VR ('The military foco must be built on the basis of a vanguard party') and the Tupamaros ('The vanguard party should be built on the basis of a military foco'). These debates are now obsolete as a consequence of efforts to overcome the party/foco dichotomy in fact and not just in theory. Among examples of convergence of vanguardist and militarist tendencies are thus the Argentine ERP ('The vanguard party currently requires a supporting foco') and Douglas Bravo's Venezuelan FALN ('The military foco should develop immediately into a vanguard party').

10 Lessons of the Bolivian Foco: The Early versus Late Guevara   SALVADORAN CP

What leaps up from the pages of Che's *Bolivian Diary*, and what Commander Guevara himself stresses in his monthly reports, is the lack of peasant support and – what is worse – the collaboration of the peasants with Barrientos' army in order to keep it well informed of the movements of the guerrilla force. If this situation is compared with the one described by the same Che in his *Passages from the Revolutionary War*, one characterized from the outset by peasant support, it can be understood that therein lies the determining cause of the defeat. It was not due to other factors, as has been alleged.

If the guerrilla force was moving toward a zone of greater political development, one may ask why it did not establish itself from the beginning in an area of this kind. The answer is found in the arrogance with which the strategy of the guerrilla foco addresses the question of political struggle and in the role it assigns to the initial nucleus as a creator of political consciousness among the masses. The strategy of the foco does not view the development of mass political consciousness as being indispensable to the outbreak of armed struggle. In the exposition of this strategy made by Debray in *Revolution in the Revolution?* we see the scheme of the German strategist Karl von Clausewitz – 'war is the continuation of the political struggle by other means' – formulated, we don't know why, in an inverted way: political struggle is a continuation of war. . . .

When the deeds are examined coldly and rationally, as they should be in all revolutionary analysis, it is seen that Che's guerrilla force in Bolivia was not part of the internal class struggle within that country. It did not represent the most advanced form of the class struggle. The old Marxist–Leninist thesis that class struggle is the motor of history in societies divided into classes, that revolution is the fruit of class struggle and thus cannot be exported or imported, that revolutionaries can only act as midwives of revolution, assisting its birth from the internal process of the class struggle, has once again proven to be a rigorously valid thesis in the light of this test in Bolivia, which is the culmination of eight years of similar attempts in Latin America. This Leninist thesis is not in disagreement with revolutionary internationalism in its highest forms – for example, the participation of combatants from one country in an armed struggle to liberate the people of another – nor is there anything vile or chauvinistic about it.

We do not pretend to lecture Fidel or, much less, to show that Che was a fool. Fidel himself, in his work *History Will Absolve Me* and in some of his speeches, has helped us and will continue to help new generations of revolutionaries to understand the connection between political struggle and armed struggle, and the historical dependence of the latter on the former. And Che has taught us in his *Guerrilla Warfare* that armed struggle can only arise and be developed after political struggle, as a means of attaining power, has been exhausted. . . .

If Che Guevara and Fidel Castro later changed their views on guerrilla war and came to originate the theory of the armed foco as the source of the revolutionary process, whether it be a foco established from within a country or one planted from without, this is a phenomenon that may be explained in terms of complex causes rooted in the social composition of the Cuban revolutionary vanguard and in the development of the Cuban Revolution after the seizure of power. . . .

As all revolutionaries, we desire the least suffering for our people, and we would seize the possibility of peaceful triumph for the revolution with all our strength if that should appear possible in practice; but, as revolutionaries, we are also realists who believe that such an eventuality is not likely for Latin American countries in general and that only exceptionally could a peaceful transformation take place in our continent. In asserting our disagreement with the strategy of the guerrilla foco, we are not, therefore, expressing opposition to armed struggle in order to take power, nor are we even questioning all forms of guerrilla warfare. We question only one form: the guerrilla foco. . . .

Epilogue by the Political Commission of the
Communist Party of El Salvador to the Salvadoran
edition of *El Diario del Che en Bolivia* (San Salvador,
1968), pp. 244–6, abridged.

11 'Guevarismo' is not 'Foquismo': The Military Foco Must be Built on the Basis of a Political Vanguard
AMÉRICO PUMARUNA

The inheritance of an improperly understood Fidelism is *foquismo*, and the classical Peruvian examples are also part of the revolutionary baggage of Latin America.

Rather than run the risk of being misinterpreted, we will explain the particular concept of *foquismo* with which this theoretical analysis is concerned. The principal idea, erroneously taken from the book of Che Guevara, *Guerrilla Warfare*, is that it is not necessary that all the conditions required for revolutionary struggle be met at the outset since the foco itself will gradually create them. But, just what concrete conditions are meant? And in what fashion should the planning and adaptation of this principle be applied to each concrete situation? These points are the ones subject to free interpretation. Naturally there are additional elements, important in presenting a rounded view of the foco. Among these are, for example, the necessity of believing in the omnipotence of the foco, which, as in the Cuban Revolution, has as its logical objectives the flight of the enemy and triumph in the midst of generalized disturbance; and the necessity that this process take place in the absence of a mass movement. A mass movement, one of the necessary conditions, does not exist at the beginning, although the hope is that it can be created during the march. In other words, all of this is explained in terms of an incomplete and defective interpretation of the Cuban revolutionary process. Many Cuban comrades are responsible for this in that they, informally, unconsciously and unintelligently, spread mistaken notions like those about the twelve men in the mountains, the superman qualities of Fidel, and the parallelism between the Sierra Maestra and the Andes. Innumerable Peruvian revolutionaries, won over by the passions of the moment and lacking in the capacity for theoretical analysis, were led to think that it sufficed to gather together twelve men (more might even be too many), to feel oneself predestined or endowed with superhuman qualities or, finally, to set up camp in any spur of the Andes in order to repeat the heroic deed of the Cuban people, who defeated Batista and in a single, uninterrupted operation brought socialism to the Glorious Isle. . . .

The Movement of the Revolutionary Left (MIR) maintained that . . . the revolutionary process would incorporate the peasant masses, students, small bourgeoisie and the working class by means of a people's war extending from the mountains to the coast, from the country to the city, and from the provinces to the capital. To achieve this the MIR chose to base itself on the 'indispensable minimum with respect to party organization and mass prestige'. Since all other energies were to be directed toward the preparation of guerrilla zones, the formation of the party was deferred and left to be done during the march. . . .

In developing the above-mentioned statements on strategy, the MIR relied on its own analysis of the Peruvian situation. The objective conditions are completely ripe; they always have been. The subjective conditions have not fully developed, but they lie beyond the leadership capabilities of the self-acclaimed revolutionary vanguards. . . .

In other words, the MIR believed that the 'indispensable minimum' for the party it had built was sufficient as an objective condition for it to act as an authentic, revolutionary vanguard, although – and everything suggests this – it never came to consider the party, whether one kind or another, as one of the objective conditions to be considered necessary. . . .

The MIR hurled itself into battle while displaying an incorrect neglect of the workers and students of the cities because the group thought it necessary to pay attention to them only in a much later stage of development. It placed too much hope in the spontaneity of these two groups, thinking that they would join the struggle and find their own place in it.

The MIR thought and maintained that the subjective conditions were sufficiently developed so that the mere presence of armed groups would suffice to mobilize the masses spontaneously and massively behind it. Because of this view, it held that the revolutionary front of highest priority was the military and guerrilla front in the country, to which MIR dedicated all its strength. The result was an evident weakness on the political front. . . .

Américo Pumaruna, *Perú: Revolución: Insurrección: Guerrillas* (Paris, 1966). From the 2nd Peruvian edition (Lima, 1968), pp. 1–2, 40–2, 44, abridged.

12 The Vanguard Party as the Political Core of the Insurrectional Foco ERP

Is the ERP the armed branch of the Party?

No. The ERP is not the armed branch of the PRT. It is a mass organization for civil war. Its ranks are composed of all Party militants and those combatants from different social classes and dissimilar political backgrounds who agree to fight for the program of the ERP. This program is anti-imperialist, anticapitalist and democratic; whereas the program of the PRT is clearly and definitively socialist. In brief, we can say that the ERP has a 'minimal' program, while the PRT pushes a 'maximal' program.

Who directs the ERP politically?

The PRT provides the political-military leadership, but its function is not simply that of an élitist army staff. It proposes to operate and grow as a political instrument amidst the masses. This project attempts to resolve some contradictions common to the Latin American revolutionary movements, among which are the problem of the 'military arm and the political arm', the antagonism between political and military actions, and the frequent estrangement of both from mass political dynamics and from the political-military characteristics of the enemy. . . .

The common criticism of armed organizations in Argentina is that military action, by its very nature, separates the revolutionaries from the masses. How would you respond to that?

That is the present criticism from a leftist reformism which is no more than a continuation of the old views of the Latin American Communist parties. The maximal expression of that criticism was that of the Venezuelan CP toward Fidel Castro.

The method of our critics consists of converting us into 'guerrilla fighters', an updated version of rural *foquismo*; but the falseness involved in distorting our strategic military position is discovered when militants from organizations that criticize us find us in factories, shops, towns and universities fighting for specific goals and taking a political position that takes into account the level of political development of the masses, but which is presented in the context of a political and military strategy that can lead to national and social liberation.

We take this position because the concept of revolutionary war as people's war requires the construction of an army which, because it is composed of armed members of the populace, must become a mass organization. This will necessarily lead to the development of a revolutionary party based on mass politics at the helm of the revolutionary war.

In addition to creating a political position for the masses, we are concerned that our combatants and militants share their everyday lives with the masses in their neighborhoods. These ties encourage the masses to accept the clandestine nature of our actions, in turn diminishing the strategic role of organizational apparatuses. In other words, it is a case of achieving an 'open' secrecy by means of political work.

Adverse criticisms would be justified with respect to the primitive sort of *foquismo*, but they have no validity when the concept they attack is that of the people operating in the middle of a war, in which the people's party acts as the center of the process.

What programmatical and organizational differences are there between the PRT *and the* ERP?

The ERP fights for a revolutionary and popular government, while the PRT (linked with the Fourth International) is a Marxist–Leninist organization which fights for a socialist government.

The only precondition for joining the ERP is the decision to combat dictatorship and imperialism. In all of the armed forces of the ERP there are 'political commissars' of the PRT who form the nucleus and are the political leaders, but these people are not always the military leaders.

What is the position of the ERP *with respect to the other armed groups that operate in the country?*

In terms of sympathy and solidarity, we have a positive attitude toward, and good relations with, all of them. Politically, we fight for a double objective:

(1) the establishment of a Revolutionary United Front to bring
together those armed organizations with a proletarian,
Marxist–Leninist and socialist perspective.

(2) the organization of another, broader front of a multiclass nature,
united by its decision to combat dictatorship and imperialism
through armed struggle.

Within this framework, common actions will be carried out by both
Marxist and non-Marxist militant organizations.

In what period of the struggle does the PRT *believe itself to be engaged?*

We are at the beginning of a revolutionary civil war, in the stage of
the propaganda of the deed, the gathering of strength, and the
wearing down of the enemy.

Naturally we expect a long war, but we are also convinced that it
has already begun, though for the moment it is being borne only by
sectors of the vanguard.

We believe that we have destroyed the city–country contradiction.
We think that there will be combat in all places where the people and
their enemy are. What is important and decisive is man, not the
terrain.

Statement by the People's Revolutionary Army (ERP)
of Argentina, '¿Qué es y cómo nace el Ejército
Revolucionario del Pueblo?', *Cristianismo y Revolución*
(Buenos Aires), January–February 1971, abridged.

13 The Military Foco Must Proceed Directly to the Creation of a Vanguard Party DOUGLAS BRAVO

As a result of the publication of Régis Debray's book *Revolution in the
Revolution*, our differences with the leadership of the Cuban
revolution increased, inasmuch as the thesis of the book was shared
fully by the Cuban comrades. The book itself did not make an
extraordinary contribution. It openly attacked what we might call
the old dogmatism, schematism, sectarianism.

But, unfortunately, because it was not based on an analysis of the Latin American reality, because it was not based on an analysis that would enable revolutionists as a whole throughout Latin America and especially in the individual countries to draw important lessons, the book fell into another kind of dogmatism. It did not formulate profound analysis but little recipes, interpretations which were in large part of a dogmatic variety.

For example, Debray's book made a myth of small groups of men, legendary figures. He exaggerated the reality that does exist. He made the question of combat, of shooting, the central point of every struggle that is going to develop at this time, brushing aside, almost absurdly underestimating, the problem of organizing the working class and the peasants and those classes which must necessarily fulfil the historic role of destroying the oligarchy and imperialism in our countries.

Debray denied the role of a revolutionary party, of a Marxist–Leninist party as the most important instrument in the liberation struggle. He denied, moreover, the role of a liberation front, basing himself on some correct arguments but reaching false conclusions.

Thus the tactic proclaimed by the book became converted into what we might call a shortcut tactic, a tactic based on the belief that the revolution in the rest of the Latin American countries was going to be made in the Cuban style and in the space of a few years. It was based on the idea that men in the mountains, paying no attention to the cities where the majority of the population is concentrated, paying no attention to other nuclei, would come down triumphant out of the hills in a few years and surround the cities.

In short, we can say that the tactic of Debrayism and of the Cuban comrades, who put it into practice in Latin America, is an incorrect tactic. It is a tactic of *foquismo*, of a shortcut, of underestimating the importance of organizing a party, a front, and of underestimating the importance of organizing the working class and the peasants.

And if we are realists we must say that things did not develop like that in Cuba, that this tactic is not the one that was applied in Cuba. It is a distortion of the Cuban experience. And this distorted version of the Cuban tactic has unquestionably produced defeats of great magnitude in Latin America. These setbacks culminated with the destruction of the guerrilla nucleus in Bolivia and particularly the death of Comandante Ernesto Guevara, which caused dismay in Latin America and throughout the world as well as in Cuba.

But once this situation had developed, which was like the crowning defeat of a tactic, what road should be taken? What road should be followed? This is what all the revolutionists of the world have been discussing. And the revisionists were delighted, saying that the road of armed struggle had failed. But we said that this road had not failed, that despite the errors that had been made, despite the incorrect, shortcut *foquista* tactic, it had been shown that the armed-struggle road was the right one for the liberation of the peoples. What had failed was a tactic, not a strategy. Therefore, what was needed was to correct the tactic in the process of the struggle itself.

Exclusive interview with Douglas Bravo published in
Marcha (Montevideo), 15 May 1970. Translated by
Intercontinental Press (New York), 8 June 1970,
abridged.

14 Military Action Creates the Political Vanguard
TUPAMAROS

What is the fundamental principle on which you have based your organization's activity up to the present?

The principle is that revolutionary action in itself, the very fact of being armed, of preparing ourselves and getting military supplies, and carrying out actions which violate bourgeois legality, generates consciousness, organization and revolutionary conditions.

What is the basic difference between your organization and others on the left?

Most of the latter seem to trust in manifestos, in the dissemination of theoretical pronouncements on revolution in order to prepare militants and revolutionary conditions, without understanding that,

fundamentally, revolutionary actions are what precipitate revolutionary conditions.

*Can you cite an historical example that shows how revolutionary action
generates consciousness, organization and revolutionary conditions?*

Cuba is an example. Instead of a long process of establishing a mass
party, a guerrilla foco is created with a dozen men and this deed
generates consciousness, organization and revolutionary conditions
which culminate in a real socialist revolution. When confronted with
a consummated revolutionary act, all authentic revolutionaries feel
themselves obliged to join. . . .

*Do you mean that the armed struggle can be engaged in the destruction of
bourgeois power at the same time that it is creating the mass movement which
an insurrectional organization needs in order to make the revolution?*

Yes, although the work put into creating a party or a mass
movement before launching an armed struggle should not be
considered a wasted effort. It is necessary to recognize that the armed
struggle hastens and precipitates the mass movement. Not only in
Cuba, but also in China, the mass party was built during the course of
the armed struggle. This means that the rigid formula of certain
theoreticians, 'first create the party and then start the revolution', has
more exceptions than applications in history. . . .

*Do you think that a revolutionary movement should prepare itself for
armed struggle in any period, even when the conditions for armed struggle are
not present?*

Yes, for at least two reasons. In the first place an armed leftist
movement can be attacked by repression in any stage of its
development, and it should be prepared to fight for its existence.
Remember Argentina and Brazil.

Secondly, if every militant is not inculcated from the beginning
with the mentality of a combatant, we will end up becoming
something else: a mere movement of support for a revolution that
others will carry out, for example, but not a revolutionary movement
in itself.

*Can this be interpreted as scorn for all other kinds of activity, other than
combat preparation?*

No, mass-organizational work that leads the people to revolutionary positions is also important. An essential point is that the militant, including the one operating on the mass front, must be aware that, when the armed struggle erupts, he is not going to be at home awaiting its outcome. He must be prepared, even if his present militancy is being conducted on other fronts. This attitude, furthermore, will add authority, authenticity, sincerity and seriousness to his present revolutionary statements.

What are the specific tasks in the mass movement of a militant who belongs to your organization?

If it is a case of a militant in a union or other mass organization, he should try to establish a circle of people, whether it be a part of the union or the whole union, which can organize support for the actions of the armed apparatus and from which members for the armed organization can be recruited. Theoretical and practical training and recruitment are the principal concrete tasks of this circle. Propaganda for the armed struggle is another. And, whenever possible, the union should be led to the most radical and definitive stages of class struggle. . . .

Don't you believe that the armed apparatus should be subordinate to a political party?

I believe that every militant apparatus should form a part of a mass political apparatus at a determined stage in the revolutionary process; and, in the event that the latter does not exist, the military arm should help create one. This does not mean that it is obliged, within the present context of leftist organizations, to affiliate with one of the existing parties or to establish a new one. . . . It is necessary to recognize that there are true revolutionaries in all the parties of the left, and many more who are not organized. To take these elements and groups wherever they may be and to unite them is a task for the left in general. This will be accomplished when sectarianisms are left behind, and it does not depend on us alone. In the meantime, the revolution cannot stop to wait for this unification to come about. Each revolutionary and each revolutionary group has but one duty: to prepare to make revolution. As Fidel said in one of his recent speeches: '. . . with a party or without a party'. The revolution cannot wait.

Clandestine interview with a member of the
Tupamaros, '30 preguntas a un tupamaro', *Punto Final*
(Santiago de Chile), 2 June 1968, abridged.

15 The Revolution Has No Need of a Party at This Stage of the Struggle   *ELN*

The following are some of the arguments used against our struggle. Guerrilla warfare has lost strength because it has had many failures in Latin America; and in Bolivia its most important exponent failed (understanding 'failure' to mean the death of Che). Guerrilla war is an élitist struggle and is thus separate from the masses. It encourages repression directed against the workers' movement and weakens the legal political work of leftist parties at the same time that it strengthens rightist intentions to carry out a *coup d'état*. Yet another argument is that revolution cannot be exported, with the insinuation that guerrilla warfare is the result of Cuban exportation.

We respond that armed struggle, basically guerrilla war, has proven itself to be the most effective method in Latin America and in the world for the gradual destruction of imperialism. It is a war of attrition for the enemy and one of reinforcement for the revolutionary camp. It is true that guerrilla warfare has suffered many defeats, particularly in Latin America, and that the only significant victory is the glorious Isle of Liberty. However, it is equally true that the struggle has only recently begun and that not all beginnings are successful. Until fifteen years ago the Communist parties were scarcely a problem for Yankee imperialism, but today the nightmare of guerrilla warfare allows it no rest. Imperialism is uncertain everywhere, and is trying to counteract the revolutionary actions of the people. It provides antisubversive schools in Panama, antiguerrilla manuals, military advisors, arms shipments and CIA agents. We see its ministry for colonial affairs, the OAS, vomiting up resolutions that condemn terrorism and guerrilla war.

Despite their defeats and lack of cohesion, the liberation movements are growing in influence – especially in Bolivia, where the mere announcement of struggle is creating polarizing effects.

All is not defeat. Guatemala is victoriously fighting for its liberation in a popular war that has greatly weakened Yankee operations.

In Brazil the guerrilla struggle received and continues to receive the approval of the people, who are joining the revolutionary war in increasing numbers. This war is carried out defiantly in the mountains.

The glorious example of the Tupamaros in Uruguay has made a profound impression not only on the Uruguayan people, but also on all of Latin America.

In Bolivia Che's 'death' definitely showed the effectiveness of a method, guerrilla warfare, and the supremacy of a theory, the guerrilla foco. It may seem ironic, but here we are to prove it.

These are examples of the effectiveness of guerrilla warfare, which has entered a new stage of revolutionary struggle.

Guerrilla war is a struggle of the vanguard, not of an élite; and its ties with the people are directly related to the interests it defends and the ideology it maintains. What have the parties, in their 'political struggles' and with their 'ties with the masses', ever done for the people during the many decades in which they participated in the government or worked in the opposition? The results speak for themselves, and we do not have to make the point.

The ELN, throughout the period of its reorganization that followed the assassination of Che, has done much better political work than any organization had done in decades of proselytization and 'consciousness-building'. The best and the most honest among the youth find that the ELN is an effective tool for liberation. The proof can be seen in that all the signatories of this document have been militants in a variety of political movements – Christian Democracy, both the pro-Moscow and pro-Peking CP's, independent Catholic groups, etc. – and have found the inertia of these party organizations to be incompatible with revolutionary obligations. Our kind of political work is the best means of silencing critics who accuse us of subordinating the political question to the military.

We do not reject the party as a means of organizing the proletariat. In a later stage we plan to establish a party that will lead the way to socialist revolution; but present conditions preclude the methods and forms of the traditional parties. The conditions now call for the formation of a political organization with a fundamentally military structure. The ELN fulfils this temporary function and will adopt new organizational forms in accordance with the levels and stages in the war for liberation.

Manifesto of the Bolivian Army of National Liberation
(ELN) 'Volvimos a las montañas', *Pensamiento Crítico*
(Havana), No. 44, September 1970, pp. 172–3,
abridged. Originally published in *Punto Final* (Santiago
de Chile), No. 109, 4 August 1970.

b DIFFERING INTERPRETATIONS OF A CONTINENTAL WAR OF LIBERATION

Two fundamental issues underlie the principal interpretations of Che's continental strategy: first, whether the leadership of the continental revolution should be assumed by Cuba as the first liberated territory of the Americas (Collazo, Bravo) or by the most important 'irradiating' focos in countries still struggling for national liberation (Peredo, Revolutionary Co-ordinating Committee); second, whether a continental strategy should serve as a catalyst of the struggle for national liberation in each country (Collazo, Bravo) or should emerge after, rather than before, these national struggles of liberation (FAR). The interpretation given by Collazo in Uruguay and Bravo in Venezuela hinges upon an analysis of Latin American reality as a Balkanized nation of twenty artificial republics; that of the Argentine FAR, on the belief that Latin America constitutes a family of nations bound together by ties other than strictly national ones; that of Peredo and the Revolutionary Co-ordinating Committee, on a composite picture of Latin America as a nation of nations, in which the unity of the Latin American nation is affirmed along with the national integrity of the separate republics. Within Guevarist circles the third or middle ground now generally prevails, although Debray's negative assessment of the ELN for underestimating the role of Bolivian nationalism and Fidel's positive assessment of nationalist tendencies within the Peruvian military junta have also strengthened FAR's position, aimed at subordinating a continental strategy to national struggles within each country.

16 The Task of Uruguayan Militants is to Join the Revolutionary Columns in Neighboring Brazil and Argentina   ARIEL COLLAZO

Uruguay may be the country in Latin America with the fewest geographic preconditions for armed struggle and rural guerrilla war.

Why, then, do we affirm that both are possible? Why do we believe that we are not an exception, as Debray maintains in his book *Revolution in the Revolution*?

It can be demonstrated by studying our history that whenever there were revolutions in Uruguay, they never developed within the country alone, in isolation, but rather in the adjoining countries. Thus, an isolated Uruguay is impossible today; it is an integral part of the continental struggle.

Because of its geographic characteristics, our territory is conducive to the rapid movement of troops from one border to another. It was for this reason that the Spaniards and the Portuguese alternated in the occupation of our land seven times during an interminable dispute over the ownership of a fortress located at Colonia del Sacramento. . . .

What is the message to be derived from the study of our past wars? It is that the geographic features always compelled the armed groups to organize in the neighboring countries, which served as operational and support bases for incursions into Uruguay. . . . Almost all of our armed struggles were initiated by means of expeditionary forces, invasions or landings organized in either Brazil or Argentina; and this has been a constant in our revolutions and civil wars. . . .

There are facts in our time that help confirm our position. In September of 1965 the gorilla generals, Costa e Silva and Onganía, who, significantly, were to become the dictators of Brazil and Argentina shortly thereafter, proclaimed that there were no longer any geographic frontiers, only ideological ones, and that the counter-revolutionary force would not be confined within each country but would expand throughout the continent. It was to be considered a single unified front against the so-called 'communist menace'. . . .

There is nothing more erroneous today than the archaic position of some Latin American leftist parties, which still maintain that the struggle should be carried out on a country-by-country basis, and also complain of intervention in their affairs by leftist organizations from other countries or by other fraternal parties.

If the gorillas are uniting, it becomes all the more urgent that the people unite in armed struggle and not simply in meetings and declarations. If the gorillas proclaim their right to intervene in any country, then the people must also intervene in struggles from country to country. If the gorillas contend that the geographic boundaries imposed in earlier times by the colonialists and the imperialists have disappeared, then with much greater reason should the peoples of the hemisphere abolish them. There are no frontiers, nor should there be any, for the people.

It is no longer acceptable to call a Uruguayan a foreigner with respect to an Argentine, a Colombian in comparison to a Cuban, or a Brazilian to a Peruvian. The only foreigners in Latin America are the Yankees who lead our armies, train our police and dominate our governments. Venezuelan, Ecuadorian, Chilean, Uruguayan and Argentine brothers and sisters must unite in the revolutionary struggle to throw the *gringos* out of our land forever. This unity is today being nurtured in the heart of the continent, in the Latin American guerrilla movement, in which patriots learn the art of war and meet the most poverty-stricken people in our poor America. While sharing their sufferings, they create a brotherhood that is only established in the struggle itself, a brotherhood that will form the basis for the future union of the Latin American republics. . . .

The continental struggle opens our country to immense possibilities. The peculiarities and obstacles of an isolated Uruguay, which led Debray to think that we were an exception, will be overcome in the struggle. Once integrated within the struggle, we Uruguayans will cease to be an exception.

In the first editorial of the *Revista América Latina* of the Uruguayan Revolutionary Movement (MRO), appearing in April of last year, we provided a thorough analysis of the Uruguayan problem which we still believe to be an accurate appraisal. . . .

'Our Movement last year proclaimed Fidel Castro as the Commander-in-Chief of the Latin American Revolution; and thus Che symbolizes today the glorious column that has left general headquarters to traverse mountains and plains in order to smash the continent-wide gorilla dictatorship.

We Uruguayans will also have a place in the forthcoming struggles. We will collaborate physically and materially with our brothers at the same time as we create bases for the future armed forces of the Uruguayan revolution.

This tactic will enable us to participate in the struggle to liberate the people of Brazil and Argentina, without which any Uruguayan liberation will be impossible.

Within the future armies for Latin American liberation, there will be one or more Uruguayan columns, which will return some day to their native soil to guarantee the laws that Artigas established in 1815, but which were violated by an imperial army – the precursor of the Yankee marines of today.'

Ariel Collazo, 'El Uruguay no es una excepción',
Pensamiento Crítico (Havana), No. 6, July 1967, pp.
103–9, abridged.

17 With Tupamaros Aid a New Bolivian Foco was Launched   *CHATO PEREDO*

Comrades of the MLN (Tupamaros):

This is to make those relations official which are already firmly established in deeds by the beautiful and magnificent solidarity displayed by you, even though these relations may have begun with the lamentable fall of a comrade.

I wish to stress the invaluable significance of the assistance you have given to our movement. We say invaluable because that aid enabled us to accelerate our return to the mountains – not to mention the moral incentive it implies for all of our combatants.

This is the beginning of a process of integration on an international level that will facilitate the destruction of imperialism. It is also an indication that not only the enemy is capable of uniting, but that revolutionaries too can erase artificial boundaries. The ideas of Bolívar and Che are beginning to bear fruit.

In the immediate future we have to give more and more, in a rapid and practical way that you find convenient. We believe, furthermore, that this kind of international solidarity should be made public so that it may serve as an example.

We are aware of the importance you assign to leading the struggle as an expanding or 'irradiating' foco directed toward all Latin American countries. We believe that this foco has its limitations, apart from your will and ours, and for that very reason we are convinced that it is necessary to open another foco in the mountains with characteristics of struggle distinct from the one you have initiated with responsibility and forethought.

Our foco will also be an irradiating and polarizing force, and it will become more so as we work together in a reciprocal manner.

These are sketchy and sweeping plans. During the course of our common work in war, these concepts will be taking form and will become more clearly defined. In the meanwhile the enemy is attacking and we must strike back. The glorious Tupamaros have become an example for us and for all revolutionaries. We shall try to emulate you in other terrains. All of our combatants extend their affection and admiration to all militants of the MLN. Victory or death in the mountains.

Chato Peredo,
for the General Staff of the ELN

Letter by Chato Peredo to the Tupamaros National
Liberation Movement (MLN), *Granma* (Havana),
1 August 1970.

18 *Latin American Guerrillas Form Joint Committee*
MLN-ERP-MIR-ELN

The Movimiento de Liberación Nacional (Tupamaros) of Uruguay, the Movimiento de Izquierda Revolucionario of Chile, the Ejército de Liberación Nacional of Bolivia, and the Ejército Revolucionario del Pueblo of Argentina have signed the present statement to inform the workers, poor peasants, urban poor, the students and intellectuals, the native peoples, and the millions of exploited workers in our martyred Latin America of our decision to join together in a Junta de

Coordinación Revolucionaria (Revolutionary Coordinating Committee).

This important step is a response to a deeply felt need, the need to offer our peoples organizational cohesion, to unite the revolutionary forces against the imperialist enemy, to achieve a greater effectiveness in the political and ideological struggle against bourgeois nationalism and reformism.

This important step is the concrete realization of one of the main strategic conceptions of Comandante Che Guevara, the hero, symbol, and pioneer of the continental socialist revolution. It is also a significant step in reviving the fraternal tradition of our peoples, who succeeded in uniting and fighting as one man against the oppressors of the past century, the Spanish colonialists. . . .

This is the final awakening of our peoples that has brought millions of workers to their feet in a process heading inexorably toward the Second Independence, toward complete national and social liberation, toward the complete elimination of the unjust capitalist system and the establishment of revolutionary socialism.

But the revolutionary road is not an easy or simple one to follow. We must not only face the barbarous economic and military force of imperialism. More subtle enemies and dangers lie in wait at every turn for the revolutionary forces, threatening their efforts to wage the anti-imperialist and anticapitalist struggle effectively and victoriously.

Today, considering the particular situation of the continental revolutionary process, we have to point specifically to two tendencies in thought and action that gravely obstruct the revolutionary efforts of Latin Americans. One is an outright enemy – bourgeois nationalism. The other is a false conception in the people's camp – reformism. . . .

Reformism . . . is a tendency rooted in the toiling population itself that reflects the fear that petty-bourgeois sectors and the labor aristocracy have of confrontation. It is characterized by a categoric rejection in practice of resorting to just and necessary revolutionary violence as the fundamental method of struggling for power and thus by an abandonment of the Marxist conception of class struggle. Reformists propagate among the masses harmful pacifist and liberal notions. They prettify the national bourgeoisie and the counter-revolutionary armies and constantly seek alliances with them. They exaggerate the importance of legality and parliamentarianism. One of their favorite arguments is that we have to avoid violence and link up with the bourgeoisie and 'patriotic officers' in order to find a peaceful road that will spare the masses bloodshed on their path toward socialism. It is an argument that has been refuted in the most painful way by events. Where reformism has been able to impose its conciliationist and pacifist policy, the enemy classes and their armies have carried out their greatest massacres against the people. The nearness of the Chilean experience, in which more than 20,000 working men and women were murdered, makes further comment unnecessary.

Against bourgeois nationalism, reformism, and other less important tendencies, in constant ideological and political struggle with them, an armed pole has emerged, a revolutionary pole that is consolidating its position daily among the masses, improving its political and military capacity, offering more and more of a real option for national independence and socialism.

It was precisely to help strengthen this revolutionary pole on a continental scale that the four organizations signing this statement decided to form the Junta de Coordinación Revolucionaria. And we call on the entire workers and people's revolutionary vanguard in Latin America to close ranks around this Junta and around each of its component national organizations in order to wage a united struggle.

This means of course that the doors of this Junta de Coordinación are open to the revolutionary organizations in the different Latin American countries.

Joint statement by Uruguay's National Liberation Movement (MLN-Tupamaros), Argentina's People's Revolutionary Army (ERP), Chile's Movement of the Revolutionary Left (MIR) and Bolivia's National Liberation Army (ELN) from Buenos Aires, 13 February 1974. Translated by *Intercontinental Press* (New York), 11 March 1974, pp. 283–5, abridged.

19 Differences with Fidel Castro Concerning A Bolivarian War of Independence   DOUGLAS BRAVO

Cuba had become an example for all self-sacrificing persons, for all those struggling for freedom. It had become a habit for the peasants and workers, the students, intellectuals, to listen to Radio Havana because the orientations and political lines were expressed in these broadcasts. A language was spoken which had not been heard since 1917, when Lenin and Trotsky addressed the peoples of the entire world with the language of the working class, with the new style of revolution. The language of Comandante Fidel Castro had a real impact on everyone in Latin America.

But after October 8 [1967], after the death of Comandante Ernesto Guevara, and a little before, a marked letdown occurred, which we noticed, which the whole world noticed. Radio Havana, Comandante Fidel Castro no longer addressed their people to inform them, to analyze, to engage in dialogue.

A letdown was natural when Comandante Guevara died. But it was also natural to expect that the man who was at the head of this army of the poor, this army of the humble, this continental army, this Bolivarian army, would say something to his troops, to the struggling people. Were we to continue on this path? Or rectify it? Or come to a halt? . . .

We maintain that the Bolivarian conception is fully valid for this epoch, that most of its postulates are still applicable. But I am going to take up only one aspect, liberating a single country. When a country succeeds in expelling the oppressors from its territory, when a country succeeds in putting the revolutionary forces in power – I am referring to a Latin American country – then it can be said that that country is in the vanguard of the rest of the army continuing the struggle. And, as the vanguard, it must march in step with the rest of the forces in the battle. This liberated country can in no way set up its own individual strategy within its own frontiers.

The liberated country must follow the strategy of the rest of the continent. Because this continent, divided up into more than twenty republics, is one single nation, which has been split up for the purpose of looting it, to make it easier to exploit it. This would be as if, in the concrete case of Venezuela, the comrades in the plains managed to liberate that area and then wanted to build socialism there, isolated from the eastern and central parts of the country, from Zulia and the Andes. Out of necessity the liberated area in the plains would have to be a base of operations for continuing the struggle.

This is true of Cuba, which has already been liberated. Liberated Cuba is only the first base of operations on the continent, from which the battle against imperialism and the oligarchies can spread more effectively. Therefore, we think, and this is what has worried us, that the line followed in practice since Comandante Fidel Castro's January 2 speech, when he spoke of putting the emphasis on production, on what he called the Year of Decisive Endeavor, is a line which is not related to the strategy of revolution, to the strategy of liberating this great nation of Latin America. . . .

Comandante Fidel Castro indeed discussed important things in this January 2 speech. He talked about the aid the socialist camp, and especially the Soviet Union, has given him. That is true, that is obviously true. The existence of a powerful worldwide socialist camp is a guarantee that a small country can build socialism within its borders today. That is real. But also, comrade, it must be recognized that these ten years of socialism in Cuba were also possible because the entire population of Latin America, 270,000,000 people, gave their support to Comandante Fidel Castro.

The people of Latin America gave Comandante Castro their fervent support in all areas and in all forms. So in making his balance sheet of these ten years, Comandante Fidel Castro should have included somewhere the contribution of these Latin American peoples, the contribution the guerrillas made with their lives, with their struggles. Because when a guerrilla dies in Guatemala, in Venezuela, in Brazil, or in Bolivia, he is not fighting for his own little country alone, for its small frontiers, he is fighting for all of Latin America.

Exclusive interview with Douglas Bravo published in *Marcha* (Montevideo), 15 May 1970. Translated by *Intercontinental Press* (New York), 8 June 1970, abridged.

20 Toward the Nationalization of the Struggle against Imperialism   FAR

Could it be said that there is a process of nationalization of the foco, nationalization in the sense of including the elements that form a real social entity with which one is to work, be it a political reality or of another kind? Do I correctly infer from what you say that it is a question of not using preconceived tactics or methods? If that is the case, would you not be close to the premise that every revolution invents its own methods to achieve its goals?

That is correct. Furthermore, every revolution should free itself from the prestige of the previous one, from that which characterizes it in some manner. That apparent paradox between what a revolution teaches and what it does is precisely the gauge for measuring the theoretical capability and the depth of vision of a vanguard.

Did Che meet these requirements?

Yes. One might say, if it were not so foolish to pass judgment at this point on a giant like Che, that to some extent Che suffered the consequences of his own experience, without intending to. . . .

Do you mean that he was exposed to two different revolutionary experiences and that the last one, in Bolivia, could not be distinguished from the other, in Cuba, which was to some extent repeated?

What complicates the analysis of Che's role is his international dimension. You recall that joke he told to the puppet ambassador to the UN who said that Che's language was neither Cuban nor

Argentine. Che said he was right, that it was Latin American – which was a serious joke. In other words, Che was extranational in dimension, and an extranational strategy is difficult at this stage. We can say that in a certain way Che was ahead of time with respect to our history, but the direction he set will inexorably become continental.

Would you say that he initiated a continental perspective that paved the way for strategies that would be more precise and more circumscribed to individual national exigencies?

Yes, I would say so.

I would like us to speak a bit more about your experience, perhaps after discussing the topic of Che, in order to see how you evaluate your experience and goals in the present situation. How about a few points of information? Having already familiarized myself with the origin of your organization, I would like to know what activities you carried out after the time you began to act autonomously; in other words, when you ceased to be economically and politically dependent on other countries.

As I was telling you, the detonator for our action was the 'Cordobazo' and related happenings from May to September of 1969. That mass violence (formidable, but like all mass violence without a vanguard, discontinuous) committed us and constitutes a mandate for us.

Excuse me, but had you not done anything before the 'Cordobazo'?

Before the 'Cordobazo', we had carried out small operations of an expropriatory nature, but of minimal military importance. After the 'Cordobazo', you might almost say that destiny was awaiting us. You will recall that shortly after Córdoba, Nixon imprudently sent as his ambassador that great boss of US monopoly capitalism in our lands, Rockefeller. We were at that time a small coalition of groups that had gathered together in Argentina for the purpose of establishing ties with and assisting Inti Peredo, who, as you recall, picked up Che's banner and also suffered an unfortunate military defeat. This shows how slow we were in drawing the correct conclusions, which we recently talked about, and reveals the extent of a certain inertia which kept us tied to a rather haphazard international adventure. We are not ashamed to admit this, but it does show how lacking we were in fundamental organizational goals and how uninvolved we were in the first stage, which is the national task. As I was saying, we formed a part of an organization composed of small groups, among which the national question was beginning to be discussed in a positive way. And the 'Cordobazo' succeeded in nationalizing us. It was a great step toward nationalization, an invaluable lesson for us. With that organization of small groups to which we belonged, we chose to respond for our people to the presence of Rockefeller and we burned a chain of supermarkets owned by him. I don't remember the number right now, but I think there were thirteen or fourteen. It was a beautiful act in which we were able to use our experience accumulated in the previous stage. It was a very important political thrust, as you probably know; so much so, that it compelled us to ponder seriously the responsibility of armed groups with a political-military capability of creating expectations that we were not in a position to satisfy.

Interview with a leader of Argentina's Revolutionary Armed Forces (FAR), December 1970, *Cristianismo y Revolución* (Buenos Aires), No. 28, April 1971, pp. 58–9, abridged.

c COMPARATIVE IMPORTANCE OF URBAN AND RURAL GUERRILLA WARFARE

Among Che's successors the debate over the comparative importance of rural and urban guerrillas crystallized into three novel theses which transcended his own limited commitment to rural guerrilla warfare: first, that rural guerrilla warfare is decisive but must begin with urban guerrillas (Marighela); second, that rural and urban guerrilla warfare are alike vital (Paquita Calvo Zapata); third, that urban guerrilla warfare is decisive (Tupamaros). The upshot of this discussion was that hardly anyone in 1974 defended Che's original thesis that the fundamental terrain of armed struggle is in the countryside.

21 Rural Guerrilla Warfare is Decisive but Begins with Urban Guerrilla Actions CARLOS MARIGHELA

There may be several political-military tendencies since Action for National Liberation (ALN) is not the only group maintaining that position. Therefore, how do you deal with the problem of a unified command?

In the first place, our strategy, which is for revolutionary war in Brazil (and I insist upon that last word), is not something closed or definitively established forever. Its fundamental orientations are clearly defined: urban guerrilla warfare, rural guerrilla war, a war of mobility, an alliance between armed forces, workers and peasants, the tactical and complementary role of the city struggles combined with the struggles in the countryside. All of this is the strategic basis. The organizations today fighting with arms in their hands agree upon this strategy, although not all view the development or stage of the struggle with the same eyes. But they fight; and it is in practice that points will be clarified, that an ever greater unity of strategy will be created and, thus, that a unified command will be established. That will never happen if people just sit around a table. A command born out of mere discussion would be artificial and would shortly disintegrate.

You have distinguished three stages: preparation for guerrilla war, igniting and implanting the struggle, and the transformation of the guerrilla war into a war of movement. Which of these have you now reached?

We have entered the second phase. The first included the formation of armed combat groups, the conversion of the permanent political crisis into a military situation, and the pressure on government generals to confess that the revolutionary war had really begun. The urban guerrilla war is implanted, and the rural guerrilla struggle will be unleashed this year. We have announced this in order to disperse the enemy, which is organizing antiguerrilla forces in several regions of the country. Those regions, and only those, does the enemy know well. We shall not go there.

Why should you begin with urban guerrilla war?

Under the dictatorship in our country propaganda work is possible initially only in the cities. Mass movements, especially those organized by students, intellectuals and some groups of union militants, have created in the major cities a favorable political climate for a harsher struggle (armed action). The antidemocratic measures taken by the government (the closing of the congress, suppression of elections, the expulsion of over one hundred senators and deputies, censorship of press, radio and television) and the innumerable acts of repression against students, professors and journalists have created a climate of rebellion. The revolutionaries have achieved the complicity of the general population. The clandestine press is advancing. 'Pirate' broadcasts are well received. The cities manifest the required objective and subjective conditions for successful guerrilla struggle. The situation in the countryside is definitely less favorable. The rural guerrilla struggle should follow the urban, which has an eminently tactical role. Furthermore, the combatants who will fight in the countryside will have been previously tested during the course of the urban war. The most valiant of those battling in the cities will be the ones sent to the countryside. . . .

Who are the rural guerrillas?

Their ranks will be formed by people born in the country who have come to the city to work. They have been politicized and trained in the city; and now they will return to their homes. The rural exodus, important in Latin America, is a positive factor from our point of view. The incorporation of the peasants into the revolution is also indispensable if we are to transform profoundly Brazilian society. A struggle which only places the urban proletariat in opposition to the bourgeoisie can lead to a compromise. It wouldn't be the first time that the urban proletariat was integrated into the system. . . .

Will the rural guerrilla come forth simultaneously in several parts of the country?

Yes. We will attack both the large Brazilian and the US landowners. We will kidnap or execute those who exploit and repress the peasants. We will take the cattle and produce from the large estates in order to give them to the peasants. We will dislocate the rural economy but will not defend any particular zone, territory or anything of the sort. To defend is to end up being defeated. As in urban guerrilla war, it is necessary that we maintain the initiative at all times and in all places. Offense is victory. Another essential point is mobility. Mobility is necessary to escape encirclement and repression and, thus, to maintain the initiative. . . .

Do the continental dimensions of Brazil favor your strategy or not?

They favor it. In our country colonization was achieved along the coastal areas, where today the repressive forces of bourgeois power (troops, arms, courts, prisons) are established. From the central areas to the west these forces are very weak. Strategic encirclement of this expanse from the coastal areas would be virtually impossible. Great natural obstacles, such as rivers, mountains and forests, separate the coastal band (about five hundred kilometers in width) from the central areas. Also Brazil borders upon countries in which the guerrilla struggle is already established. The continental dimensions of Brazil do not favor the application of the foco theory, but they do favor our strategy of revolutionary war.

Exclusive interview with Carlos Marighela, September 1969, *Front* (Paris), No. 3, November 1969. Spanish translation in *Pensamiento Crítico* (Havana), No. 37, February 1970, pp. 94–7, 99–101, abridged.

22 Urban and Rural Guerrillas Have the Same Importance   *PAQUITA CALVO ZAPATA*

The armed struggle recently begun in Mexico is a result of the maturation of revolutionary consciousness, antidemocratic repression, and the spontaneity of the mass struggle.

I firmly believe that the armed struggle is, on one hand, the maximum expression of political consciousness and, on the other, the result of the absence of an organized mass vanguard. It is not the only revolutionary approach, but rather one of several. It is necessary for the following reasons: (1) in a tactical sense, as a means of pressuring the government and, with respect to the masses, of building consciousness and organization and of setting off a political explosion at the proper time; and (2) in a strategic sense, as part of the combined struggles to create a revolutionary power capable of enduring and overcoming repression, of maintaining and perfecting its own organization and of confronting reactionary forces in order to take power.

I will now state the political-military objectives of the Zapatist Urban Front (FUZ). To begin, I would like to point out that, given the very special characteristics of our country with respect to the rest of Latin America, both urban and rural guerrilla warfare have the same importance and are equally necessary. Urban guerrilla struggle is being developed in the urban industrial centers, in the large cities where the population is concentrated and political conflicts are heightened to the maximum.

In the semifeudal countryside, with its masses of peasants who have been pauperized and a thousand times deceived, rural guerrilla struggle will find – and has in fact already found – all the support it needs to establish an invincible revolutionary force. This support is evident in the cases of the Peasant Brigades of the Poor People's Party and of the commandos of the Revolutionary National Civic Association (ACNR). We have chosen urban guerrilla struggle, but we also concede the same degree of importance to both fronts. We proposed, as a first step, the organization and consolidation of a front for urban struggle. At the time of our detention, the front was composed of an armed command and an open command. The armed command carried out military actions and functioned as the political-military leader of the front. The open command was responsible mainly for the organizational work of recruitment. The objectives of the military actions executed by the armed command were: (1) to provide sufficient economic resources for the organization; and (2) to awaken popular consciousness.

The actions were both political-economic, as in the expropriation of the bank and the kidnapping of Hirschfeld, and one hundred per cent political, as in the cases of the distribution of money among the people and of the sentencing and punishment of corrupt politicians, infamous exploiters and assassins of the regime. The purpose in expropriating the bank was to symbolize the recovery of money belonging to the people from the hands of one of their worst exploiters: finance capitalism. With respect to the kidnapping of Hirschfeld, we tried to demonstrate that the millionaires and representatives of private enterprise work hand in glove with government functionaries and, also, that there exists an alliance between the powerful 'revolutionary' families (Aarón Sáenz, Elías Calles . . .) and the former groups. The three hundred thousand pesos distributed among the people represented a symbolic return to the people, although in meagre portions, of part of the money stolen from them by government and private enterprise. In other words, the fundamental objective of the armed command was to build consciousness. When we reached a certain level of growth, the internal chain-of-command structure for the organization had already been prepared and foreseen. The next objective after the consolidation of the urban front was political and military co-ordination with all other urban and rural guerrilla organizations, a first step toward unification in a massive organization for armed struggle on a national level. . . .

The alliance between the national organization for armed struggle, on one hand, and the democratic mass national organization of the revolutionary vanguard, on the other, may not be able to take state power in certain situations, but it will constitute an organized revolutionary force which acts in accordance with the overall strategy of the Latin American struggle. In my opinion, this process, which leads to the formation of an organized revolutionary force that combines both the armed and the democratic struggles, is in fact taking place in Latin America today. We see its most evident manifestations in Uruguay, Chile and Argentina. It is beginning to take place in Mexico, principally in spontaneous fashion and secondarily in a conscious way.

We guerrillas of Latin America are no more than a symptom, an indication of humanity's great step toward socialism, of the transition from the capitalist to the socialist mode of production. Our sole intention is now and has been to create the subjective conditions for the Latin American socialist revolution, to hasten its arrival. That is all.

Prison interview with Paquita Calvo Zapata, member of the Zapatist Urban Front (FUZ) of Mexico, *Punto Crítico* (México DF), June 1972, pp. 28–9, abridged.

23 Urban Guerrillas as the Main Force of the Revolution
TUPAMAROS

At this point, I would like to return to the second part of my question, that concerning the urban nature of the armed struggle.

I'll begin by saying that the decision to take the way of armed struggle was in no way dependent on the specific geographical characteristics of our country. It is a matter of concept. Otherwise, those countries lacking the geographical conditions favorable to rural guerrilla warfare, for example, would have to discard armed struggle in the process of revolution.

There was a time when the urban guerrillas were looked upon as units to provide logistic support – communications, weapons, funds, etc. – for what should be the main nucleus: the rural guerrillas. This concept was discussed by the MLN on the basis of an analysis of our national situation – in which the possibilities for rural guerrilla warfare are practically nil, since we have neither vast jungles nor mountains – and some previous experiences, and we came to the conclusion that the development of urban struggle was possible, thanks to some very interesting, specific conditions.

We studied the French resistance to Nazi occupation; the Algerian struggle – which, even though it developed mainly in the mountains, had its counterpart in the cities; and an example which, as a result of its methodology, its being strictly limited to the urban areas, was extremely useful to the Movement: the struggle waged by the Jews against the English, reference to which is made in a booklet entitled 'Rebellion in the Holy Land'.

On the basis of these facts, it was considered feasible to begin the experiment in Latin America of a guerrilla force whose action would be centered in the cities instead of in the countryside.

Comparatively speaking, what are the advantages and disadvantages, as far as your organization is concerned, of urban and rural guerrilla warfare?

We believe that urban struggle has a number of advantages over rural struggle and that, in turn, the rural struggle also presents certain advantages over the urban struggle. However, the important thing, at this stage of the game, is the proof that the nucleus can come to life, survive and develop within the city, and all this in keeping with its own laws. It is true that we are operating right in the mouth of the enemy, but it is also true that the enemy has got us stuck in its throat. We are faced with the inconvenience of having to lead a dual life, in which we carry on a public activity – whenever we are able to – yet, in reality, are somebody else altogether. But we have the advantage of having a series of indispensable resources at hand which rural guerrillas must engage in special operations to obtain: food, ammunition, weapons, and communications. The same thing applies with respect to the environment: our adaptation to it comes almost naturally.

Adaptation to the environment is another interesting factor. We, the urban guerrillas, move about in a city which we know like the palm of our hand, in which we look like everybody else and where we go from one place to another with the same ease as do the other million people who live in it.

However, the rate of our losses, in relation to our experiences in Montevideo, shows a marked increase. Every week, every two weeks, every month, the number of comrades who are captured increases. Were it not for a very strong Tupamaros–people relationship, this might mean that the organization would be decimated. . . .

Hasn't the organization, in view of the specific conditions that exist in Uruguay, thought of reversing the usual roles and developing some type of rural guerrilla unit that would serve as support or complement to the urban guerrilla action?

The tactical plan contemplated by the organization at present includes extending the war to the interior of the country. A series of actions that were planned recently, which included cutting off communications – tearing down telephone poles, etc. – have been carried out. Many of these actions will eventually be planned within the characteristics of the urban struggle. In other words, even though these actions will be carried out in the countryside, they will have characteristics not so much of rural guerrilla action but rather of a commando raid – that is, going out, completing the operation, and returning, if possible, to normal everyday life.

Exclusive interview with a leader of the Tupamaros
National Liberation Movement (MLN), 13 October
1970. English edition of *Granma* (Havana), 18 October
1970, p. 11, abridged.

d THE RESPONSE TO BROAD FRONTS AND POPULAR GOVERNMENTS

The question of how to respond to broad fronts and popular governments is currently the most controversial and least resolved issue dividing Guevarist movements in Latin America. Although there is virtually no disagreement concerning support for broad fronts against reactionary military and civilian regimes – the position of the Dominican CP is representative on this score – fundamental differences have arisen in response to broad fronts and populist movements in power. The Peruvian MIR has consistently opposed the nationalist-populist military junta of President Velasco, whereas Héctor Béjar, speaking for the remnants of the Peruvian ELN, switched from an original strategy of opposition to one of support. The Bolivian ELN continued to oppose the populist-military regime of General Torres even after the inauguration of the Popular Assembly on May Day 1971, coming to the government's defense only with the launching of the military coup in August of that year. In Argentina a Peronist broad front assumed power in May 1973 following a landslide victory at the polls, in response to which the FAR suspended armed actions as a token of support for the new government while the ERP continued its attacks on the reactionary armed forces and multinational corporations. And in Chile, where a unique kind of popular coalition emerged based on a united front of the Socialist and Communist parties, the MIR shifted from a position of nonparticipation to one of militant support for Allende in power, and then to active opposition in August 1973 – a month before the military coup – on the ground that the government had already capitulated to pressures from the right.

24 The Regrouping of Forces behind Bosch's Thesis of 'People's Dictatorship'   *DOMINICAN CP*

Our Party has not been free of internal struggles. Within our ranks an ideological battle was fought arising from the process of self-criticism and resulting in the resignation of a group of members of the leadership who held positions opposed to the adoption of an independent international policy. These comrades defended the positions of the Communist Party of the Soviet Union (CPSU) unconditionally and established a party assuming the name we originally used: the People's Socialist Party (PSP).

For anyone observing our political situation from the outside, it would seem that the revolutionary war was like striking a loosely tied bundle, scattering helter-skelter the forces that made up the front. Up to a certain point, when seen from the outside, the breakup of some parties could give rise to that judgment, and we must point out some of the factors that oblige us to see the question not as a simple phenomenon of dispersion, but rather as a regrouping of forces. We are faced with the resounding failure of all political lines that do not interpret our national reality and that, therefore, do not offer any practicable solutions – those of both theorists and pragmatists.

It has not all been dispersion. New forces have come out of the experiences in the armed struggle against the invader. On the national scene, the main protagonists – Juan Bosch, representing the most advanced ideological current within the Dominican Revolutionary Party (PRD), and Francisco Caamaño, an Army man who headed the constitutional government of the city of Santo Domingo – are both exponents of the inverse movements of regrouping, of uniting the people around the urgent problems of the revolution.

Our Party attributes the leading of our country's transformation at this time to this tendency toward the cohesion of the strongest democratic and anti-imperialist forces. For us, this is a truth which springs from our organizational experiences, since the number of members and friends of our communist organization has increased and extended throughout the country. . . .

In the face of the political scene that was unfolding, it was necessary to reach conclusions as to the nature of the regime and to define a corresponding opposition policy. The Dominican Communist Party considered that the regime imposed on us through fraudulent elections controlled from Washington served to give the intervention a façade of nationalism while maintaining its counterrevolutionary essence. This conclusion could only lead to calling for the overthrow of the government. It will be necessary to present a solution in accordance with the demand for a complete, revolutionary transformation of the traditional oppressor institutions. This then calls for the establishment of a government similar to the one headed by Francisco Caamaño during the siege of the city of Santo Domingo. . . .

This question of what the methods for the revolution should be is not very controversial for the Dominican people. We have gone through the experience of a civil war and know that the enemy is stubborn, that it will never peacefully give up its oppressor state. If the electoral farce that brought Joaquín Balaguer to the Presidency has served any purpose at all, it is that of teaching the people the uselessness of this means for overcoming the deep-rooted evils that afflict them.

Based on that experience, our Party and the main forces of the constitutionalist movement which faced the Yankee armies in 1965 subjectively prepared and are continuing to prepare the masses for new violent clashes, for revolutionary war. The watchword of armed struggle guides all truly nationalist and democratic policy.

Juan Bosch – the overthrown democratic President who is today the principal leader of the PRD – with deep respect for history accepted the challenge and recognized that in the Dominican Republic any regime established to defend the interests of the people would be incompatible with the monopolies. Such a regime must come about as the result of a fierce struggle against the monopolies. That position was established in his thesis of 'People's Dictatorship' as the political solution when the liberation struggle ends victoriously. The fact that a man such as Bosch, who had firmly believed in the possibility of establishing a democratic government that would maintain cordial relations with the US ruling class under the traditional republican form, has now assumed such a radical position is indicative of the great advance in the people's thinking.

Statement by the Dominican Communist Party, 'Santo
Domingo: The Watchword of Armed Struggle',
Tricontinental (Havana), No. 9, November–December
1968, pp. 55–7, abridged.

25 A United Front with the Peronist Movement in the Struggle against Imperialism   *FAR*

The people's camp . . . is made up of the industrial working class as
well as other urban and rural workers, the greater part of the student
and intellectual sectors, broad sectors of professionals and the poorest
sectors of the rural and urban petty bourgeoisie (small scale
businessmen, industrialists and agricultural producers). The workers,
because of their social importance, experience in struggle, level of
consciousness, and the fact that they are the only ones who have taken
up a revolutionary perspective, are those who make up the principal
force of this camp and who must also be its leading hegemonic
force. . . . The program of the people's camp is not absolutely anti-
bourgeois; *it is essentially anti-imperialist, antimonopolist and anti-
oligarchic,* as the first step in the transition to socialism. . . .

Peronism's revolutionary sectors are themselves in the minority at
the policy-making level of government. They must orient themselves
toward obtaining more influence within the Movement and the
Government in such a way that the people's interests are faithfully
represented in their superstructures. Their gaining of a hegemonic
position will be the best guarantee for the uninterrupted development
of the liberation process and the achievement of the transition to
socialism. . . .

We have maintained that the objectives of the people's camp
should be set in accordance with their capabilities (political,
ideological and organizational) and should take into consideration the
enemy's ability to impose his contrary interests. In other words, the
objectives that the people's camp sets itself in each period must relate
to the balance of forces that exists in that period and to their possible
development.

A revolutionary politics does not set ambitious objectives that cannot be attained with the forces available to advance them. . . .

A revolutionary politics is one which proposes to achieve the maximum objectives possible in accord with the forces at its disposition; one which formulates attainable objectives; one which step by step is able to increase the forces in the people's camp and diminish the enemy's; one which definitively builds people's power and destroys the power of the dominant classes. . . .

What, then, is the balance of forces between the people's camp and the enemy in the conjuncture beginning May 25th? What are the possible objectives that the people must consider?

We have already spoken about the situation in the enemy camp, about its limited political force, its economic strength and its relative military weakness. Although it is somewhat obvious to point this out, this camp is supported economically and militarily by imperialism.

The people's side has great political strength in its favor which gives it the overwhelming majority character that was reaffirmed in the March 11th elections. This massiveness, however, lacks sufficient organization and preparation. This error began to be revealed when the politico-military organizations appeared in the movement; but their development is still not sufficient to conquer the enemy armed forces militarily.

In spite of this limitation, at present *the people's camp is on the offensive*. But the objectives of this offensive are not unlimited. They are what makes the present balance of forces possible. The enemy [forces] are pulling back, but they have not been annihilated. Are we now able to annihilate them totally? We believe not. Despite their present weakness, if we are to rout them totally, to annihilate them, we ought to have a military force superior to theirs and we still don't have it. . . . Until this happens, elementary wisdom counsels avoidance of a total armed conflict and in its stead the waging of only limited fights.

Document issued by Argentina's Revolutionary Armed
Forces (FAR), May 1973. Translated in NACLA's *Latin America
& Empire Report* (New York), September 1973, pp. 24–5, abridged.

26 Support for Allende's Government of Popular Unity Requires a Change in the Immediate Objectives of Armed Struggle   *MIR*

In obtaining an electoral majority, Popular Unity (UP) has formalized an impasse between the dominant classes and the workers, while establishing the theoretic rights of the left to assume government control. This electoral majority of the left has led to an alignment of forces which has formalized, on one hand, the aspirations of the workers to become the government and, on the other, the decision by the controlling classes to defend their interests. Both, in reality, are preparing for a confrontation that sooner or later will resolve the impasse.

The UP is attempting to become the government by virtue of the electoral majority it won. In accordance with the circumstances that prevail today in Chile, a leftist government entails the occupation of the public offices of the Presidency, Ministries, etc., by members of the UP. As long as the state apparatus, its bureaucratic and military structure, remains intact, the UP cannot go beyond that point. The apparatus will continue being an instrument for control and will continue to represent ruling-class interests. As Lenin said, those who really govern are the immense body of middle-ranking functionaries, technocrats, bureaucrats and military figures in the ministries, subsecretariats, corporations, etc. – those who can only be replaced by revolution.

The possibility for a 'government of the left' to progress toward more advanced phases depends on: (1) whether or not the apparatus of the capitalist state is destroyed; (2) the nature of the participation of the masses in the process; (3) the revolutionary composition of the political forces leading the struggle; and (4) the means adopted in the fight against imperialism and financial, industrial and agrarian capitalism. If the foregoing characteristics insure a revolutionary orientation, then they will necessarily lead to a military confrontation between the ruling classes and the workers. . . .

We have always affirmed that the taking of power by the workers will only be possible through warfare. . . . Nevertheless, we have also maintained that the armed struggle will take form as a prolonged and irregular revolutionary war and that it will not be a popular insurrection which in a few hours will definitively place power in the hands of the workers. We say this because, despite the setbacks suffered by imperialism in the Vietnamese War and the advances made by the anticolonialist revolution throughout the world, imperialism is still immensely powerful, as are the indigenous ruling classes in Latin America. Only an irregular war, which in its political and military development gradually weakens the ruling classes and strengthens the revolutionaries, can be successful in Chile.

Nothing with respect to these fundamental conditions has been changed by the electoral victory of the UP. The confrontation has only been postponed. When it does take place, it will be more legitimate and will be characterized by massive popular participation – all of which make the strategy of armed struggle more important now than ever before. . . .

It is apparent that necessary changes will have to be made in concurrence with the political situation of the country and the opportunities, content and form of our kind of struggle. All tasks in these areas should be presently directed toward defending the electoral triumph of the left and fighting extreme rightist organizations. Later, on the mass fronts, the task will be to carry out the program. . . .

The composition of the UP, its relative weakness and that of the revolutionary sectors, imposes two possible alternatives. One is to bow to pressures from the Christian Democrats and other mummies and to 'stabilize' the future government. The other is to mobilize the masses in order to demand their right to govern and to impose their conditions, even if this should lead to a confrontation of classes. The Christian Democratic junta and the agreement by the UP to form the required Commission lead one to believe that Allende will assume power without a conflict. However, we should not dismiss the possibility that circumstances difficult to foresee might provoke a conflict (an attempted assassination of Allende, a series of attempted assassinations by the extreme right, the international situation, etc.). Even with the UP governing and even, in fact, with it acting as a 'stabilized' government, it is still possible that political or economic measures, even nonradical ones, might provoke a reactionary and imperialist counteroffensive. That, in turn, might lead the government to rely to a greater extent on the worker and peasant movement; and, thus, a radicalization might occur that would precipitate an historic confrontation.

We believe that the workers have already won the right to convert into property of the people foreign firms, banks, factories and agricultural enterprises. The people have already elected Salvador Allende President; and that is a non-negotiable item. The basic task at present is to defend the electoral victory from the maneuvers of the bourgeoisie and the imperialists by encouraging mobilization of the masses within their organizations and by formulating a policy with respect to subofficials and military personnel. We will bring attention to the dangers inherent in the effort to take power for the workers via the electoral route and will seek to prepare the people for the confrontation that this course necessarily implies. . . .

We will maintain our political-military structure for as long as capitalism reigns in Chile and power has not yet been achieved by the workers. The defense of the workers' interests will continue to be our sole justification for existence.

Declaration by the National Secretariat of Chile's
Movement of the Revolutionary Left (MIR) on the 1970
electoral results, *Punto Final* (Santiago de Chile), No.
113, 13 October 1970, abridged.

27 Exceptions to Fidel's Assessment of the Peruvian Military Junta

HÉCTOR BÉJAR and RICARDO GADEA

Héctor Béjar and Ricardo Gadea were interviewed by the *Intercontinental Press* while they were in Lurigancho Prison. Béjar is the author of the essay *Perú 1965: Notes on a Guerrilla Experience* (Sandino Press), which won an award by the Casa de las Américas in 1969. He represents the position of the Army of National Liberation (ELN). Ricardo Gadea speaks for the position of the Movement of the Revolutionary Left (MIR). Both Gadea and Béjar were active militants in the guerrilla conflict of 1965.

What do you understand the relation between the party and the revolution to be?

BÉJAR: I do not believe it is necessary to have a party in order to make a revolution. In Peru there are many revolutionary organizations. In the present-day movement there exists a division of labor among them. For example, the Front of the Revolutionary Left (FIR) has worked among the peasants; the Revolutionary Vanguard (VR) among students and workers. The Maoists are working with students and peasants. In this sense, the party is already there. It is true that there is no unified direction, but I don't believe that is possible at present.

To attempt to create a party now with a unified direction, before working for the revolution, would create an obstacle. We need freedom of expression for all tendencies in the movement, and a party would set us back. . . .

GADEA: It is true that there are a series of organizations with some common objectives and also with different views. We are in a developmental stage with respect to a party.

In my opinion the party will be created in the process of revolutionary struggle. I disagree with those who think they can form a party and then proclaim themselves 'the vanguard'.

I belong to the MIR. We launched a Marxist movement. We don't consider ourselves the vanguard but rather a part of the vanguard.

We believe that all revolutionary groups should remain completely independent of the government. The present government is a bourgeois-reformist regime, a capitalist regime. Revolutionaries and the proletariat of Peru must prepare themselves for a real revolution. There is no other way. The task for the present is political and military preparation, and in order to accomplish this the left must participate in the mass movement. The left is weak today. While it works to strengthen itself, it must remember that its objective is war, revolutionary war. In organizational terms we should prepare to fight with weapons.

We need to work among the masses in order to strengthen ourselves and to encourage a combative spirit among the masses. This is our immediate task. Every revolutionary must be imbued with the conviction that at a given moment he will be a combatant and that the organization will count on him to hurl himself into combat. Our entire effort should be dedicated to the preparation for a future revolutionary situation. . . .

What do you think of the speech by Fidel Castro in which he accepted the possibility that the military regime might lead the Peruvian revolution?

BÉJAR: I believe that Fidel is mistaken. The Peruvian army will continue to be a bourgeois army. This is not a dogmatic assertion but an expression of the real situation, indicated by the actions of the government against us.

GADEA: We disagree with Fidel. We recognize the fact that Cuba has for many years maintained an internationalist revolutionary line toward Latin America. The MIR itself is proof of this. However, the MIR has been from its origin an independent organization linked to the realities of its country.

The truth about the present government is that it is not revolutionary. Its reforms are directed toward strengthening the development of monopoly capitalism. This process will not lead to the liberation of our country but rather to increased dependence. This is perfectly clear. Since handing over copper to the United States via the 'Open Door' policy toward foreign investments, this tendency has been accelerated.

Prison interview with Héctor Béjar and Ricardo Gadea,
Revista de América (Buenos Aires), May 1970, pp. 22–4,
abridged.

28 Why We Do Not Support the Popular Government of General Torres   *ELN*

For three days, starting Sunday, October 4, when General Miranda attempted an ultragorilla coup, the country was the spectator of disputes and deliberations among the different military bands. This situation gradually became defined in favor of the revolutionary nationalists, who, after the resignation of Ovando, and under the leadership of J. J. Torres, sought backing among the popular and progressive sectors. Thus, with popular support, the gorilla coup was frustrated, and Torres was able to take over the Presidency with the promise of a popular revolution.

The problem with which we are presented now is that of discovering what can be expected of this government. Evidently, the country needs a thoroughgoing revolution to recover the wealth of the nation from the hands of importers, exporters and foreign corporations and concentrate all our productive resources to meet the needs of the people and development. It is very clear that any serious attempt to carry out such a transformation involves the socialization of the economy. However, powerful interests oppose this kind of change. The present economic, social and political structures, which are responsible for underdevelopment and misery, are based on the principal factor in any Latin American regime: the Armed Forces. This military caste subsidized by the Pentagon has, in General Miranda, a monstrous example of the reactionaries who hide behind its commanding officers. As long as this powerful caste exists as the possessor of arms and power, saturated at its higher levels with gorillas with personal and family ties to imperialist interests, no revolution is possible. . . . Therefore, the problem to be discussed is whether or not General Torres and his government can carry out a genuine change in structures.

There are a series of indications that lead us to give a negative answer. . . . The repeated aim of preventing an armed clash with the gorillas entrenched in the General Staff Headquarters . . . leads us to assume that within this group of officers there still prevails, above their populist intentions, a caste spirit which – because they are members of the Armed Forces, whose unity they wish to safeguard – makes them shy away from the physical annihilation of the worst enemies of the people. . . .

The lack of definitions of the structural changes that are supposedly desired and the absence of serious attempts to do justice by annihilating the reaction, the enemies of the people, the gorilla military, are indications, in our view, that the nation's steady deterioration under the Ovando government will very likely continue under the present one. The reaction, whose economic and military bases of support have been left intact, will again lift its head and put pressure on the Government until it makes it betray its principles, or it will instead overthrow the Government when popular enthusiasm declines as a result of the lack of definition of those holding power. The historic lesson on this point is conclusive: without exception, reformist regimes are unable to annihilate the reaction and, thus, they either fall or end up by betraying their reformist aspirations. There are more than enough examples of this: Perón in Argentina, Vargas in Brazil, Paz Estenssoro in our country, Arbenz in Guatemala, Bosch in the Dominican Republic, Nkrumah in Ghana, Sukarno in Indonesia and Sihanouk in Cambodia suffered the consequences of their fence-sitting or lack of long-range political insight.

In the present circumstances the people cannot be appeased with the reformist formula, whose well-known results we have been seeing since September 1969.

The ELN has not chosen its strategy of prolonged war because of any romantic notion, mechanical copy of other experiences or simple dogmatism. We believe that a genuine revolution presupposes the physical annihilation or expulsion from the country of the reactionary forces through armed struggle. This task can only be carried out by all the people, as a whole, when their level of awareness, organization and political and military experience qualify them to do so. The capacity of the popular masses to take power cannot arise overnight, as if by magic, nor can it be the fruit of spontaneity, as many of those who favor a putsch would believe. Our organization maintains that the only way to achieve this in the present historical circumstances is to begin a prolonged revolutionary war, in which the fighting vanguard, through its example, makes possible the growing awareness and incorporation into the struggle of ever-broader sectors of the popular masses.

Communiqué by the National Liberation Army (ELN) on the situation in Bolivia, 10 October 1970. English edition of *Granma* (Havana), 18 October 1970, p. 12, abridged.

29 The Government Has Capitulated! Why the MIR No Longer Supports the Popular Unity Coalition of Salvador Allende   *MIR*

The government has significantly capitulated before a sector of the ruling class. That is the simple and crude truth. This truth should be proclaimed without any disguises to the Chilean people and to the people of the world.

The hopes once placed in this government by the dispossessed masses of our country are beginning to crumble.

The castle of illusory words with which impotent reformism and craven centrism sought to hide their failure is collapsing. The dream of class collaboration has turned out to be a gimmick to disarm the masses. The harsh reality is now apparent: a sector of the bourgeoisie has imposed important conditions and will continue to demand more; reformism has surrendered and is now unmasked before the eyes of the people.

Perhaps someone will say that we exaggerate. Nevertheless, the exploited masses will rapidly begin to understand, as victims, the tragic meaning of the word 'capitulation'.

It is necessary to call things by their proper names and not to continue deceiving – ever again – the working class and the people. The government has significantly capitulated, and that is the truth.

The government has not been strengthened. In truth, only the bourgeois state, the power of the bosses, has been strengthened. . . .

What objectives does the sector of the ruling class seek in this cabinet? The division and confusion of the people, with the help of reformist complicity; in other words, better conditions for a rightist coup.

To affirm, then, that the installation of this cabinet represents a strengthening of the government is not only a lie but something much worse. It is an attempt to disguise the truth and to apologize for the step backward in order to deceive the masses, to disarm them and hand them over, tied hand and foot, to the bosses. Apart from the efforts to survive or the concessions to be made within the cabinet to the representatives of bourgeois order by reformism or centrism, what is perfectly obvious is that this cabinet greatly facilitates the plans of one sector of the bourgeoisie to restore the bourgeois state – even though this aspect of the situation may be momentarily obscured by the tremendous aggressiveness of the other sector which seeks a coup. . . .

The working class and the people must know that henceforth they can no longer rely upon an additional tool in their struggles. The formation of this cabinet should place the working class and the people in a state of constant alert. They should issue a proclamation on the formation of this cabinet concerning which they were not consulted. The masses must denounce all attempts by this cabinet to boil down their class conquests. Leftist militants must profoundly meditate the meaning of this cabinet and be disposed to examine its leaders ever more critically. The working class and the people must realize that the only means to resist the return of firms and agricultural enterprises to private ownership is to create an instrument for combat that responds directly to their own interests: People's Power. Revolutionaries should consider the installation of this cabinet as the final signal to regroup the revolutionary forces. The working class and the people must be immediately transformed into thousands and thousands of activists for this cause, for unity with honest soldiers, sailors, guardsmen and officers.

The working class and the people must understand that the only hope for victory resides in a revolutionary and popular counter-offensive and in the implementation of those means of struggle most suited to the present circumstances. Revolutionaries must succeed in using the present conditions to their advantage in order to unmask reformism before the masses and thus to build a solid revolutionary bloc that will secure victory for the workers and the people.

Editorial, 'El Gobierno ha capitulado', *El Rebelde*
(Santiago de Chile), No. 95, 14–20 August 1973,
abridged.

Part Three

*The Impact of
Guevarism on Third World
Liberation Movements*

a A TREND WITHIN THE CUBAN REVOLUTION

In this document Che's thesis of the parallel and simultaneous development of both productive forces and revolutionary consciousness is given a novel interpretation by Fidel: the parallel construction of socialism and communism. Although material incentives are necessary to stimulate production – hence the rationale for the socialist principle of payment according to work – the sacrifices required by a communist principle of distribution are necessary not only to care for the needy, but also to develop the new man.

30 Cuba's Little Heresy: The Parallel Construction of Socialism and Communism   FIDEL CASTRO

I repeat that, logically, all things are not free because that would only be the case in a communist society. Of course we speak of formulas, socialist formulas and communist ones; and it is said, in accordance with the formulas, that in a socialist society each person works according to his ability and is compensated according to his work, and that under communism everyone labors according to his ability and receives according to his need. However, I ask what would we do in this stage of building socialism in the case of a widowed woman with seven children, whose work capacity is negligible. If she were compensated for her work, it would be absolutely impossible for her to feed and clothe her seven children. Can the socialist state ignore the suffering of her seven children? Can it allow them to be raised shoeless, rickety and undernourished simply because we wish to apply to this woman the formula with respect to work, thus forgetting her necessities or waiting for the arrival of communism to apply the formula with respect to need? Of course not! We cannot wait. The woman would suffer, the children would suffer; and that would be cruel. Furthermore, society would suffer because it is concerned with the growth of healthy citizens. Every human being must have the necessities for a decent existence – especially a child.

All of this, of course, demonstrates that no formula can always be literally applied and that, generally speaking, formulas in political and social matters are always bad. . . .

We are developing our ideas. We understand that Marxist–Leninist ideas require incessant development; and we understand that a certain stagnation has taken hold in this area. We also observe that sometimes formulas are universally accepted which diverge sharply from the essence of Marxism–Leninism.

We believe that the construction and development of socialism and the march toward a superior society, communism, must necessarily have laws and methods and that, naturally, these methods can never be the same as those of capitalist society. We believe that our laws and methods are not based on blind laws or on automatic regulations. They must increasingly be based on the ability of the people to plan in order to control the processes of production, to anticipate and foresee; in other words, to direct and to control those laws, but not to become puppets manipulated by them. . . . On a certain occasion, with respect to the formation of the Central Committee, we said that we did not believe that communism could be built in complete independence from socialism, that communism and socialism should be developed, to a certain extent, along parallel lines. We felt that it would be a grave error to invent a process and to say: 'We build socialism up to this point, and we build communism after that.' We would add that, in the midst of striving to attain socialist goals, the development and creation of the communist man should never be renounced or left to the distant future.

When I expressed all of this, it was not, needless to say, the opinion of a schoolteacher, an apostle, a professor, an authority on revolutionary theory or, much less, of some kind of little ideological Pope; but some people were astounded. Quite a few readers of manuals were astonished and quite a few – I say this not because I have counted them, but because I estimate their number by those who were not pleased by this affirmation – quite a few people who are accustomed to having their ideas as well arranged as the clothing in their closet were disturbed even by this affirmation; and I do not doubt that some might have wondered whether we were uttering sacrilegious opinions.

From Fidel Castro's May Day 1966 speech, *Discursos pronunciados por el comandante Fidel Castro Ruz . . . en distintos actos celebrados desde 1965 a 1968* (Havana, 1968), pp. 46–8, abridged.

b THE INFLUENCE OF GUEVARISM ON THE ESTABLISHED CP'S

Within the established Communist parties the influence of Guevarism on the younger generation has resulted in the following types of organizational change: (1) split between a party's armed apparatus and its central committee over the issue of military initiatives versus the reduction of the armed struggle to an instrument of political bargaining (Guatemalan FAR)*; (2) organization by* CP *cadres of an armed movement independent of the party's political direction (Nicaraguan* FSLN)*; (3) expulsion of the party's left wing for organizing armed actions in defiance of the political apparatus (Communist Group of São Paulo); (4) split by the right wing in response to a radicalization of the party's leadership (Honduran* CP)*; and (5) rupture by the left wing leading to the organization of a rival or revolutionary* CP *(Argentine Revolutionary Communist Party). As a consequence of these organizational changes almost all of the established* CP's *are now comparatively free of Guevarist tendencies.*

31 From a Political-Military Alliance with the CP to an Independent Movement of National Liberation
CÉSAR MONTES

At an especially critical moment for the Guatemalan Revolution, at a time when the civil war is most intense and when the internal crisis in the revolutionary movement has reached its climax. . . , guerrilla leaders of the Edgar Ibarra Front (FGEI) and of the Resistance of the Central Zone have, in the name of the Rebel Armed Forces (FAR), taken on the historic responsibility of publicly breaking all organic and ideological connections with the Workers Party of Guatemala (PGT) and have established the FAR command as an independent centralized organization. . . .

The need for this break was foreseen by the FGEI in its charter in October 1964 and has almost become fact several times since then. This was a process of divergence at first, and later of dispute, between two ideas, two attitudes toward the war, toward the Revolution, toward the people, both determined by deep class roots and a historic moment. On one side there is the revolutionary idea, which sees war as the people's instrument and method for taking power into their own hands so as to liberate themselves and make their revolution: the socialist revolution. Therefore it is not subject to the fear that this may be a total war, long, bloody and generalized. This is a radical vision, revolutionary, audacious, young, dynamic. On the other side is the pseudo-revolutionary idea, which does not believe in the people's ability to take power into their own hands; which has confidence in the ability of the bourgeoisie to direct a democratic regime of state capitalism progressing peacefully, evolving tranquilly toward socialism. It is, therefore, a concept that opposes war, is wary of the possibility of winning such a war, prefers a road of successive displacements of the bourgeois factions in power until the arrival at some combination which gives the left influence, participation in the government. Under the pressure of events and popular feeling, this concept can go so far as to accept a limited, small-scale war, static and indefinite which, in addition, it would try to use as a political argument to make the bourgeoisie recognize its right of participation in the government. . . .

In none of the events that have shaped a course and have determined objective phases and advances in the still brief history of our revolutionary guerrilla war, a chain of positive features typifying our Revolution, has the initiative, foresight, inspiration or organizational contribution of the PGT leadership been present, except for the founding of the FAR and the Provisional Center of Revolutionary Leadership (CPDR) of the FAR, in which it had to participate due to the initiative of other forces; and, in any event, its contribution was to hold back and deflect the momentum and original objective, and not to stimulate and develop it. . . . It has been of no assistance. It has been a tremendous stumbling block. Now it will not continue holding us back from within, and we will not allow it to do so from outside.

Statement by César Montes, Commander-in-Chief of
the Rebel Armed Forces (FAR) of Guatemala,
21 January 1968. English edition of *Granma* (Havana),
3 March 1968, p. 11, abridged.

32 Organization of National Liberation Fronts Independent of the Party's Direction
CARLOS FONSECA AMADOR

For many years Marxist influence in the opposition to the Somoza regime was extremely weak. The anti-Somozaist opposition was almost totally controlled by the conservative sector, a political force which represented the interests of part of the capitalist class. One of the causes for the weakness of the Marxist sector had to do with the conditions under which the Nicaraguan Socialist Party (traditional communist organization of Nicaragua) was constituted. That organization was founded in June of 1944, when the Second World War was still not over, and the theory of Earl Browder, Secretary of the Communist Party of the United States, was in force, a theory which proposed conciliation with the capitalist class and with US imperialism in Latin America. . . .

The period from the assassination of Sandino in 1934 to the triumph of the Cuban Revolution in 1959 had as its principal characteristic the interruption of the traditional armed struggle as a systematic tactic to combat the ruling regime. Another principal characteristic was the almost complete domination the conservative sector exercised over the anti-Somozaist opposition. This situation, which lasted for 25 years, preceded the new stage which began with the armed struggle of the Cuban people and their victorious revolution. . . .

It should be said that, for some time, more exactly from 1962 on, various armed actions were undertaken by different groups. This reflected the complete anarchy from which the insurrectional revolutionary sector suffered. The Sandino Front of National Liberation (FSLN) resolved that problem, when it became the political and military instrument.

From 1959 to 1962 the illusion was maintained among the components of the FSLN that it was possible to achieve a change in the pacifist line of the leadership of the Nicaraguan Socialist Party. In 1962 such an illusion disappeared practically, with the construction of the Sandino Front, an independent grouping, although for some time thereafter the idea was maintained that it was possible to reach a certain unity with the Nicaraguan Socialist Party leadership, an idea which reality had to refute. . . .

The Sandino Front of National Liberation considers that now and for a certain time Nicaragua will be going through a stage in which a radical political force will be acquiring its physiognomy. Consequently, in the present moment it is necessary that we emphatically state that our greatest objective is the socialist revolution – a revolution to defeat Yankee imperialism, its local agents, the false opposition, and false revolutionaries. This propaganda, with the consistent backing of armed action, will allow the Front to win the support of a sector of the masses conscious of the depth of the struggle we are carrying out.

The force the capitalist parties represent through the influence they still exercise in the opposition must be taken into account in order to plan the strategy of the revolutionary movement. It is necessary to be alert to the danger that the revolutionary insurrection could serve to escalate the reactionary force of opposition to the Somozaist regime. The task of the revolutionary movement is twofold. On the one hand, to overthrow the criminal and traitorous clique that for long years has usurped power, and, on the other, to prevent the capitalist force of the opposition, with its proven submission to Yankee imperialism, from taking advantage of the situation opened by the guerrilla struggle, to seize state power. In the task of ousting the traitorous capitalists, a revolutionary, political, and military force with roots among a broad sector of the people must play a singular role. . . .

As for the Nicaraguan Socialist Party, it can be said that the changes in leadership of that political organization are solely changes in form. The old leadership creates illusions regarding the conservative sector and calls for the construction of a political front in which these stalwarts of imperialism occupy a place. The so-called new leadership currently justifies having participated in the electoral farce of 1967 supporting the pseudo-opposition candidacy of the conservative politician Fernando Agüero. Just like the old leadership, the so-called new leadership never ceases to speak of armed struggle, while in practice it concentrates its energies in legalistic work.

Carlos Fonseca Amador, 'Zero Hour in Nicaragua',
Tricontinental (Havana), No. 14, September–October
1969, pp. 32–3, 35, 40–1, abridged.

33 Left-Wing Factions within the Established CP's Expelled for Organizing Armed Actions
CARLOS MARIGHELA

With the pronouncement made public by this document, we wish to set forth our viewpoint on the way to lead the armed struggle in Brazil.

Belonging to this group are communists of São Paulo who, due to their opposition to the pacific line, disagreed with the Central Committee (cc) and were either expelled or victimized by arbitrary measures. They had no opportunity to defend themselves since they were not allowed to participate in the meetings at which they were expelled.

The gulf between ourselves and the cc has taken on the character of a definitive separation.

This break became fully evident upon the occasion of the OLAS Conference, when the cc expressed its disapproval and applied extremely punitive measures against those who disagreed with the pacific line.

Such measures were ratified and even strengthened after the discussions at the Party's Sixth Congress, convened without notifying those who disagreed and converted into a fraud. Not even the delegates from São Paulo or their alternates were called to attend.

With respect to armed struggle, we have already stated our position on several previous occasions, affirming always that we favor the armed road to revolution.

As for the OLAS, we approve and support the General Declaration of that Conference and we are in agreement respecting the necessity to read, study and follow the directives of the final twenty points, which are fundamental to that document.

The political line of the General Declaration of the OLAS is the one we have adopted. . . .

An organization like the old Executive Committee and its organs, molded in the image of the CC, with its auxiliaries, assistants, etc., is not suited for armed struggle and, much less, for guerrilla struggle, which is an exalted expression of revolutionary war.

We now need a clandestine organization that will be small, well-structured, flexible and mobile: a vanguard organization to act, to carry out revolutionary actions on a constant and daily basis, one which will avoid getting tangled up in endless discussions and meetings.

It must be a vigilant organization that deals severely with spies and applies efficient security measures in order to avoid being destroyed by the police or infiltrated by the enemy.

The members of this organization are men and women dedicated to making revolution. The communists in this organization are comrades with a spirit of initiative, free of bureaucratic and routine tendencies, who do not wait for the so-called 'assistants' and who do not sit around waiting for orders.

Nobody is obliged to join this organization. Those who accept it and decide to form part of it do so voluntarily, because they want to be obligated to the revolution.

The democracy in this organization is revolutionary democracy. What counts is action and what one must keep in mind is the interest of the revolution, for which the fundamental duty is concrete initiative.

There are three principles upon which this organization is based: (1) the duty of every revolutionary is to make the revolution; (2) we ask no one's permission to carry out revolutionary actions; and (3) we are committed only to revolution.

This organization is beginning to be established, with a revolutionary will and without asking anyone's permission, by dissident communists and by groups and organizations unalterably opposed to the CC and its arbitrary decisions.

From this dissidence and rebelliousness arose a small co-ordinating center which now functions as a guerrilla force. Other revolutionary groups are now arising from this same spirit of rebellion and opposition.

We think the time has now come to finish once and for all with the endless internal discussions. We should waste no more time on the struggle within the CC. . . .

The communist grouping of São Paulo is opposed to the establishment of another communist party. We do not want to form another party that would return to the old arguments and become a repetition of the old party structure – all of which would be prejudicial to immediate revolutionary activity. Our strategy is to embark on a course of direct action, of armed struggle. The theoretic concept which guides us is that action makes the vanguard. It would be inexcusable for us to waste time organizing a new summit, spewing out the so-called 'programmatic and tactical' documents, calling for new conferences, from which would come another Central Committee with all the familiar vices and aberrations. Today the discussion table no longer unites revolutionaries. What unites Brazilian revolutionaries is action, and action is the guerrilla.

In preparing for action, without any disputes about this or that share of leadership, without getting involved in the affairs of other revolutionary organizations and without attempting to combine the organizations, we only try to maximize our efforts to set loose the guerrilla war. Later our duty is to make the revolution.

Carlos Marighela, 'Pronunciamiento de la agrupación
comunista de São Paulo', February 1968. Spanish
translation in *Pensamiento Crítico* (Havana), No. 37,
February 1970, pp. 3–4, 6–7, 9, abridged.

34 Radicalization of the CP's Followed by Right-Wing Splits   *HONDURAN CP*

The military dictatorship established in Honduras by the coup of
October 3, 1963, is a part of the imperialist offensive directed against
the Latin American people, aimed at greater exploitation of these
countries and destruction of their liberation movements. With the
military coup, imperialism dealt a final destructive blow to the
'representative democracy' which was incapable of protecting its
interests, and replaced it with a new regime in which the army,
completely controlled by the Yankee Pentagon through its military
mission, is the true and permanent force that determines every aspect
of national politics. . . .

The military dictatorship is the expression of the alliance between
imperialism, the middle class bourgeoisie, and the landowners. The
struggle against the military dictatorship is the form in which our
people's struggle is directed against its main enemy: North American
imperialism. It is not possible to fight imperialism, as the rightist
opportunists claim, without also fighting the military dictatorship.
Nor is it possible to fight the military dictatorship, as the liberal
leaders pretend to do, without a determined fight against North
American imperialism. . . .

The working class, the peasants, the petit-bourgeois segment, are
the moving forces of the Honduran revolution – conceived as an
agrarian, antifeudal, and anti-imperialist revolution – without
excluding the possibility of some isolated and circumstantial
collaboration from elements or sectors of the bourgeoisie which
oppose imperialism and the oligarchy. From this point of view, 'the
surrender of the democratic programs' to a supposed anti-imperialist
national bourgeoisie is an opportunistic and reactionary slogan which
has no place in the political plans for our people.

The objective that we must outline is the destruction of the military dictatorship through mass movements and armed actions as the fundamental form of struggle. This is the approach we counterpose to the opportunistic slogan of 'democratizing the regime'. . . .

The opportunists of *Voz Popular* and *Trabajo* [organs of the right-wing Communist Party] propose the 'democratization' of the government and of the army as the way to catch up with the changes the country needs. They view 'democratization' of the government and of the army as a strategic objective, from within the framework of their opportunistic rightist policies – which is the only framework they have – right up to the point where 'peaceful transition' and the 'struggle for peace' are their main activities. . . .

In the present situation . . . 'democratization' of the government and of the army is a totally unrealistic concept. But in addition to being both false and vacuous from the point of view of our situation, this 'democratization' of the government and the army is essentially reactionary. It reinforces the dictatorship and tries to create illusions among the people concerning a probable social transformation without the need for revolution. . . .

Considering a series of factors, we can say that in Honduras the guerrilla struggle is the most appropriate form of popular action, the form that most closely responds to the needs of the revolutionary movement and which holds the greatest possibility for further development and complete success. . . . Through guerrilla warfare, whose principal terrain will be the mountains, the revolutionary forces will gradually alter the balance of forces which, though unfavorable at the beginning, will eventually match those of the enemy and will conquer and defeat him. This will be a process requiring large numbers and the patient work of accumulating those forces over a long period; it will be a prolonged war. . . .

It is certain that armed actions should not be undertaken if the minimum subjective conditions do not exist – that is to say, a certain level of organization and a mass consciousness sufficient to insure the consolidation and development of the armed movement. But it is false to expect the full maturity of these conditions in a country such as ours, because the joining of objective and subjective conditions are necessities of the final battle for the immediate seizure of power, but are not essential to begin and develop an armed guerrilla struggle. . . .

In Honduras the objective conditions are sufficiently developed so that they can be joined with minimum subjective conditions which will be created by organization, propaganda, agitation, and elevation of mass political consciousness, which our Party and other revolutionary organizations have undertaken. This will permit the beginning of an armed revolutionary process which will be strengthened as it fights the enemy and embarks on the formation of a people's liberation army – a guerrilla army – a revolutionary instrument through which it will be possible to destroy the bureaucratic-military apparatus of the oligarchic and pro-imperialist state.

Statement by the Communist Party of Honduras, 'The Road of the Honduran Revolution', *Tricontinental* (Havana), No. 15, November–December 1969, pp. 13–15, 22, 35–6, abridged.

35 Emergence of New Revolutionary CP's Committed to Armed Struggle *OTTO VARGAS*

Our Party was created on the basis of the rupture that took place in the Communist Party in September 1967, spurred by the apogee of the Bolivian guerrilla struggle and the holding of the First OLAS Conference. This rupture took shape when the Central Committee of the Communist Youth (supported by the vast majority of its organizations and a number of Party groups in Buenos Aires Province and in the federal capital, Santa Fé, Córdoba, Mendoza, etc.) expressed solidarity with the attitude assumed by the Communist Youth against the positions of the traditional PCA leadership. The new Communist Party was created January 6, 1968, and precisely because it wanted to recover the revolutionary national and international tradition of Communism it named itself the Communist Party (Movement of Revolutionary Recovery).

Our Party arises from a long process operating inside the Argentine Communist Party which began with what is known in the international Communist movement as 'Browderism'. There were few Communist Parties in Latin America that carried to such a level of absurdity the ideas of 'class conciliation' and 'conciliation with imperialism' formulated by Browder, as did the Argentine Communist Party, which taught – through articles written by its leader, Vittorio Codovilla – the possibility of a so-called evolutionary way for the Argentine democratic revolution which, according to him, would be carried out 'with the cooperation of the democratic governments of the United States and Great Britain'. . . .

We believe that the fundamental force of the Argentine revolution is the proletariat; from this, comes our proposition for armed struggle that tends fundamentally to put the proletariat in motion . . . we give great importance to the experiences in urban struggle that have recently taken place, such as that in Brazil and that of the Tupamaros in Uruguay. . . .

We consider necessary the continental coordination of the struggle such as Che Guevara proposed. It is necessary to create in the Andes and along the Latin American coastal zone great centers of armed struggle as bases for the armed struggle of all the countries of the Cono Sur. We believe that the revolutionary struggle in our country has to try to lead the proletariat of the Cono Sur to struggle; in any case the proletariat of the Argentine coast, and the native and peasant masses of all the areas north of Argentina: Bolivia, Peru, Brazil, Paraguay, Ecuador, etc. In other words, the revolution in Argentina has as its main protagonist the proletariat, but it cannot triumph or consolidate itself if its struggle is not combined with that of the native and peasant masses that form the area north of our country to Colombia and Venezuela, that live side by side along the length of the Andes. . . .

We believe Che Guevara's instructions about urban struggle are valid, although we also believe that he didn't say it would be impossible to maintain well-trained armed action groups in the city capable of struggling effectively. That struggle brings forth the question of how to create these permanent military forces capable of destroying the government of the enemy classes.

We don't believe the Argentine struggle could be a peasant struggle; one has to consider that there is a wide plain with a highly developed capitalist agricultural zone on the coast, that goes from Rosario to La Plata (a little more than a hundred kilometers) that belongs to the almost two million workers that are concentrated in that area.

There is, to be sure, a zone next to the bordering countries north of Argentina where the majority of the poor peasants are concentrated, that makes the development of guerrilla zones possible – which, by themselves, can't decide the situation, but combined with the work in the cities and in the country could define it.

For us the process of armed struggle has to culminate in a general uprising of the people. Now, since we don't have the same situation that existed in the Soviet Union, where there was a world war, we can't achieve a successful general insurrection without a long process of confrontation with the state and without the creation of an army belonging to the people, capable of making this insurrection victorious.

We believe that in Argentina the working class can't engage in a struggle against imperialism except through the class struggle. That is, we believe that a worker of the imperialist meat-packing industry reaches an understanding of the anti-imperialist struggle not through the anti-imperialist struggle in general, but rather he comes to understand the role of imperialism when he collects his salary – that is, through surplus value. Therefore, we believe that the proletariat can't fully carry out its function if it is not transformed first into a revolutionary force directed by authentic socialist forces. As the traditional Communist Party has not played this role, we must try to play it.

Otto Vargas, 'Argentina: Prolegomena of Rebellion',
Tricontinental (Havana), No. 12, May–June 1969, pp.
127–8, 130, 132, abridged.

c THE GUEVARIZATION OF LATIN AMERICAN TROTSKYISM

The impact of Guevarism on the Trotskyist parties of Latin America has contributed to a change of strategy: the pursuit of permanent revolution through the organization of military focos (Martorell); the insertion of a guerrilla nucleus within peasant unions and mass political movements (Condoruma); the organization of armed detachments to combat military and civilian reformism as well as threats of a fascist coup (Bolivian POR); and the development of armed vanguards for a prolonged revolutionary war on a continental scale (Argentine ERP). Actually, Che's influence has been greater on the Latin American sections of the Fourth International (Unified Secretariat) than on any other left-wing parties on the continent.

36 Permanent Revolution through New Insurrectional Focos on the Continent   JOSÉ MARTORELL

After his visit to Peru, Daniel Pereyra and the Spaniard José Martorell Soto had a significant conversation (November of 1960) in the Argentine capital. They spoke of the revolution. Martorell gave this account of what they said on that occasion.

'I had just visited Cuba. . . . Between sips of coffee at a table in the bar I remembered . . . my conversations with Che Guevara. I was absolutely convinced that armed insurrection was the only correct approach for the countries of Latin America. I was personally disposed to defend my conviction and to put it into practice with all of my physical and intellectual capacity. . . . I was thinking about this when Daniel came in.

' "How is Cuba these days?" he asked.

' "On a war footing, to resist aggression. . . ."

' "That is very impressive. I would give my life to be in Cuba during these times."

' "I would too, Daniel. But, the fact is that to defend the Cuban Revolution it is not exactly necessary to be there."

' "I understand you. The Cuban Revolution is the beginning of the revolution in America."

' "Of course! The best way to defend it is by opening new insurrectional focos on the continent. . . ."

' "Yes, that is true; but do you mean romantically, without plans? Without a more or less effective political organization? Without a minimum of favorable objective conditions and significant contact with the masses? Please explain this better."

' "Che Guevara refers to these related conditions in his book on guerrilla war. He states that you cannot wait for conditions to mature and that the insurrectional foco helps create them . . . , which confirms that people who invoke the supposed nonexistence of favorable conditions have learned nothing from the strategic lessons provided by the Cuban Revolution. There are those who grant the existence of favorable objective conditions, but they immediately add that the subjective ones are lacking. By inadequate subjective conditions, they mean the lack of a revolutionary party, sufficiently well-developed and organized to confront the tasks of armed struggle. That is true, although not sufficient reason to disdain the tasks of insurrection. . . ."

' "All right," he responded. "I understand you. The lesson of the Cuban Revolution is that it has shown, once and for all, that the insurrectional line is the correct one. . . . A party that dreams of attaining power by means of spurious alliances and electoral agreements has nothing to do with revolution. . . ."

'After that evening encounter on Corrientes Street we talked frequently. We engaged in a serious analysis of the political situation in each and every country. We studied the real situation of the vanguard parties. We concluded that Venezuela, Colombia, Brazil, Peru and Paraguay were ripe for launching a rebellion. It was simply a matter of establishing the foco or the first guerrilla contingent. It was at this point that some key issues were discussed.

'The Cuban Revolution showed that it is possible to defeat a professional army vastly superior in technique and resources and also that it is possible to oppose successfully the pressure, sabotage and aggression of the United States. . . .

'The main problem has to do with the strength of the leftist vanguards, which must assume the task of promoting the guerrilla and terrorist forces. It is not a task for spontaneous types but rather for leaders, men in contact with the people.

'Later, at another meeting, the electoral question arose. Daniel said: "We must be implacably opposed to the electoral communist parties." And I answered him: "Which means that we must sweep away the illusions of peaceful coexistence." Daniel added: "The only way to have an impact on the people and on the communist membership is to prove to them the errors of their ways with deeds."

' "You are right," I said. "A guerrilla operation speaks louder than tons of paper. . . ."

'Such were the ideas we exchanged during a series of meetings. Our Argentine comrades of the Trotskyist tendency declared themselves in solidarity with our positions. We began to draw up plans.'

Prison notebook from Gonzalo Añi's *Historia secreta de las guerrillas* (Lima, 1968), pp. 36–41, abridged.

37 Combining Mass Political Actions and Guerrilla Warfare   *SILVESTRE CONDORUMA*

Shortly before the initiation of guerrilla struggles early in 1965, some leaders originally from diverse political groupings – the American Revolutionary Popular Alliance (APRA), Popular Action (AP), the Communist Party of Peru (PCP), MIR, FIR – but all of a Trotskyist leaning, decided to form a new organization called the Revolutionary Vanguard (VR). The declared objective of VR was to appraise critically the overall political process in Peru in recent years, and the Latin American struggle in general, in order to specify the theoretic and programmatic bases required by the latest stage in these struggles.

Since v r was displeased by both the Castroist tendency, which placed all of its emphasis on the guerrilla focos and disdained urban-rural political work, and the tendencies of the remaining groups, which placed all the emphasis on political work and postponed immediate preparation for armed struggle, v r proposed to clarify both of these positions. . . .

The unfortunate experience of the first heroic guerrilla fighters has illustrated an unavoidable fact, which must be understood and confronted in all of its implications: the revolutionary struggle in Peru cannot be developed successfully if it consists solely of guerrilla war. By the same token, the experience of Hugo Blanco and the peasant movement demonstrated that the revolutionary political struggle cannot be carried out effectively without an armed organization.

From this point on, nobody can or should think that any one of these paths, when applied in isolation, can ever lead to the capture of power and the revolutionary transformation of society. With guerrillas alone it is not possible; nor is it possible with politics alone.

If one truly strives to develop the Peruvian and Latin American revolution, with an honesty not tempered by hunger for personal power or special group interests, then it must be conceded that only a well-integrated combination of political work and armed struggle can provide for the authentic fusion of mass movements and guerrilla action. . . .

The Peruvian guerrillas did not begin prematurely; they were preceded by ten consecutive years of work with the peasant movement. However, they began without any systematic evaluation and generalization of the efforts at incorporating the guerrillas into the peasant movement. It now appears that in the future the survival of the guerrillas will not be possible unless the control of a considerable portion of the peasant movement shifts toward the revolutionary left; and that will only be possible by intensifying the peasants' struggle for the land.

In the next stage the guerrillas in the countryside will have to function as armed organizations for defense and support of the peasants' struggle, for a long period of time, until the peasants come to view the guerrillas' cause as their own. This requires the cancellation of the confrontation with the army and police and the subordination of that struggle to the defense of the peasants' struggle for land. Guerrilla actions must be converted into actions supportive of the peasant movement through retaliatory actions against large landowners and their local agents.

However, the creation of an urban-rural political movement, an organized political apparatus directing the urban student movement and the urban and semi-urban labor organizations, is absolutely necessary in order to get organized urban support for the armed struggle, to lessen the government's opportunity to concentrate its repressive efforts against guerrilla groups, and to gain influence over the imagination and aspirations of the urban masses. The latter are still influenced at present by traditional means of struggle and by populist and old left policies and ideologies.

Silvestre Condoruma, 'Las experiencias de la última
etapa de las luchas revolucionarias en el Perú', *Estrategia*
(Santiago de Chile), No. 5, April 1966, abridged.

38 A War on Two Fronts against Fascism and Reformism   *POR*

The fear of the revolutionary forces tends to accelerate plans for a coup by imperialism and military fascism. Although the Army, faced with a mobilization of workers during the October crisis, authorized General Torres to form a government for the purpose of politically disarming the masses, that same Army has now decided to get rid of Torres since its mission failed. The Army wants to return to a strong-arm policy, and the situation of the Torres Government is very precarious. Torres can no longer count on the support of the Army nor on that of the masses, who have been defrauded. Fearing revolutionary radicalization above all, he is attempting to regain the confidence of his military friends. That is the meaning of his statements to journalists, to whom he insisted that he was not a socialist but a 'nationalist', that the Bolivian Labor Central (COB) and the People's Command do not share in power and, finally, that the Popular Assembly was not a legitimate organ. The nature of the Torres Government was perfectly apparent: opposed to mobilization of the masses and in favor of their containment.

For these reasons we say that the Bolivian revolutionary process faces two perils. The first is a fascist coup, encouraged by the Yankee Embassy and the Argentine and Brazilian gorillas, a coup being nurtured in the ranks of the Bolivian armed forces. The second threat is posed by military and civilian reformism, which seeks to drug the consciousness of the masses. Reformism has in fact become an obstacle to the triumph of the revolution.

On this May Day, a day to pay homage to our proletarian heroes, we must affirm loudly and clearly that we are opposed to and will combat with arms in our hands any attempt at a fascist coup. But this position should not lead us to support nationalist bourgeois reformism. In this historic moment we are not obliged to choose among these two alternatives because we have our own path: socialism. It is for the socialist alternative that workers are mobilizing and preparing to fight until death. . . .

It is necessary to reject the attempts of opportunists and capitulators who use the fear of a fascist coup to yoke the masses to the cart of military reformism. The fascist conspiracy, in the final analysis, feeds upon the limitations and vacillations of the Torres Government. The fascist threat cannot be extirpated without first expelling reformism from power and making the socialist revolution. . . .

It is certain that the Popular Assemblies and the Political Commands of the Working Class and the People are growing. However, even when these organizations become developed as centers of expression of the will of the masses, they will remain incomplete unless accompanied by the parallel development of the People's Revolutionary Army and the arming of labor groups.

We have said that the march to socialism requires the taking of power, in effect a people's army, armed detachments of the people.

Everyone knows that he who has arms takes power. Not to understand that is to be ignorant of the dynamics of revolution and class struggle. The bourgeoisie will not passively relinquish power. We have to tear it from their hands by means of armed violence. But in order to defeat the bourgeois army, the working class and revolutionaries must create their own army.

Let us not deceive ourselves. The innumerable massacres have taught us a lesson. With that experience in mind, the POR calls upon all workers this first of May to organize their armed pickets and their proletarian and peasant regiments. In every factory, mine, peasant community, university, we must organize the armed detachments, which will be the embryo of the People's Revolutionary Army. Only thus can we smash the conspiring fascists and assault the positions of the capitalist regime. Only thus will the revolution triumph and lead the way to socialism.

Armed and organized mass mobilization is the way to defeat fascism and nationalist reformism. . . .

Glory to Che Guevara and Inti Peredo!

La Paz, May 1, 1971

May Day Message of the Revolutionary Labor Party (POR) of Bolivia, 'Marchemos al Asalto Final del Poder para el Socialismo!' *Combate* (La Paz), 1–15 May, 1971, pp. 1, 7, abridged.

39 Trotskyist Armed Units Committed to Guevara's Strategy of Liberation *ERP*

They would appreciate it if journalists would stop referring to them, for reasons of convenience, as 'Trotskyists' or the 'armed branch of the Partido Revolucionario de los Trabajadores' [PRT – Revolutionary Workers' Party]. The party defines itself as Marxist–Leninist, and considers the label 'Trotskyist' to be 'inadequate'. Although it accepts the contributions of Trotsky exposing the degenerative role of the bureaucracy, as well as his concept of world revolution and permanent revolution, and although it belongs to the Fourth International ('we think that we can contribute to proletarianizing it, but we are aware of its limitations'), it also draws on the experiences of Che Guevara (especially), Mao, Giap, Ho Chi Minh, and Kim Il Sung.

While the PRT is a Marxist–Leninist party, being a Marxist–Leninist is not a requirement for those who are active in the ERP. This armed, mass organization is certainly led by the party, but it seeks to bring together all those patriots who, whatever their ideology, are ready to fight weapons in hand for the socialist revolution. . . .

Q. *What kind of relationship does the* ERP *have with the other armed Argentine organizations?*

A. From our very inception, we have made, and continue to make, permanent appeals for unity in action among the armed re-volutionary organizations, with the aim of building a solid, strong, and unified army of the people, in which there are certainly going to be Peronist and non-Peronist fighters, but in which they will all be united by a common methodology – prolonged revolutionary war – and a common ideal: the building of socialism in our country.

On basic points we share a common orientation. We have fraternal relations with all the armed sister organizations. We maintain that all the contradictions that we have with these organizations must be characterized as contradictions among the people that must be resolved though a critical approach, without conciliation, through the ideological discussion that we are constantly calling on our brothers in struggle to engage in – without making concessions, which we ourselves have never made nor asked for – but also through seeking out points of agreement that open up common political ground; examples of this have in fact been demonstrated, in practice, by the actions that have been carried out jointly. And it is our view that the points that unite us are much more numerous than those that separate us.

Q. *How does the struggle you are waging in Argentina fit into a continental strategy for liberation?*

A.   We recognize Ernesto Che Guevara as the top commander in the revolutionary war on which we have embarked. And this is not a mere reference or an expression of personal affinity. It also stems from a general agreement with his strategic conceptions for developing the revolution: create two, three, many Vietnams, with one – or several – of them in Latin America.

Our starting point was also his concept and his exemplary practice of proletarian internationalism: to be in whatever place people are fighting imperialism arms in hand. This is the reason that our strategy is continental, that we maintain fraternal relations with all revolutionary organizations in Latin America, that we recognize the Cuban revolution as a beacon of liberation in Latin America, and that we see that liberation does not result from the development of revolutions that remain isolated in each country, but that the revolution (national because of the specific forms it adopts in each country) will have an internationalist content.

Interview with two official spokesmen of Argentina's
People's Revolutionary Army (ERP), *Chile Hoy*
(Santiago de Chile), 11–17 May 1973. Translated by
Intercontinental Press (New York), 28 May 1973, pp.
649, 652–3, abridged.

d GUEVARISM AMONG DISSIDENT SOCIALISTS

The first document in this selection marks a change in strategy by the Chilean
MIR, *organized initially by dissident cadres from the Socialist Party with the*
support of Trotskyist splinter groups. The MIR's *turn toward armed struggle*
dates from this statement by its political secretariat in support of Che's
'Message to the Tricontinental'. The second document relates how the
Tupamaros underwent a somewhat different evolution from an armed
appendage of the Uruguayan Socialist Party into an autonomous Guevarist-
type movement. Unlike the original nucleus of the MIR, *Sendic's group split*
with the SP *after, not before, taking up the armed struggle.*

40 The Chilean MIR Subscribes to Che's Message to the Tricontinental   *MIR*

The Central Committee of the Movement of the Revolutionary Left
(MIR) believes that the broad dissemination of the 'Letter from Che
Guevara' constitutes a vital revolutionary task for the future of Latin
America. . . .

It appears at a crucial moment, when the Venezuelan guerrilla
movement, led by Douglas Bravo and Américo Martín, is
overcoming the crisis caused by the desertion of the Venezuelan CP;
when in Guatemala a new insurrectional leadership guides the FAR
and the legendary figure of Yon Sosa is vindicated by Che; when in
Bolivia a tempestuous guerrilla movement breaks loose and the
gorilla leaders are attempting to have Régis Debray assassinated;
when armed insurrection is deepening its roots in Colombia; and
when the sand begins to shift beneath the feet of the military
dictatorship in Brazil.

With their military intervention in Santo Domingo, the Yankee
imperialist bandits have served notice to the countries of Latin
America that they 'will not permit the establishment of anti-
imperialist or socialist governments' in the hemisphere, under penalty

of destroying them militarily, even if that means crushing the countries' independence and their right to national self-determination. Thus it is that a hypothetical 'government of Allende' has been notified beforehand by Washington of military intervention.

When confronted with these designs, the theoreticians of 'peaceful coexistence' and of the 'peaceful' transition from capitalism to socialism stick their beards in manure and then conclude that something stinks in their theoretical concepts and in their opportunistic strategies.

It is perfectly obvious that imperialism will not die 'peacefully' and that the period of 'peaceful coexistence' with some socialist states was a mere strategic truce and a military tactic, but not a permanent standard of behavior. Latin America, the backyard of the United States, must examine its relationship to the colossus of the north from an entirely new perspective.

Che Guevara warns those who believe in peaceful coexistence that 'everything indicates that the peace, that precarious peace only given that name because no world-wide conflagration has occurred, is once again in danger of being destroyed by an irreversible and unacceptable step taken by the North Americans'. He adds: 'Since the imperialists have blackmailed humanity with the threat of war, the proper response is not to fear war.' To attack, harshly and without pause at every point of confrontation, should be the general tactic of the people. . . .

This position of Che is reaffirmed in other paragraphs of the 'Letter' in which he states that 'the strategic objective of the insurrectional struggle should be the destruction of imperialism. This authentic liberation of the people will only come about through armed struggle, in the majority of cases; and it will almost inevitably in America acquire the characteristics of a socialist revolution.' He also says that the triumph of the revolution implies the installation of a 'socialist style of government'.

The MIR has intransigently maintained this same position because it has understood that social change can only bring about national liberation and democracy insofar as it adheres to the goal of socialist revolution.

We also believe that the armed insurrectional strategy and guerrilla action will lead to the highest expression of class struggle, a struggle which until today has been limited to general strikes and street demonstrations. We believe that the national and social war will be protracted and harsh.

Until recently the mosaic pattern of Latin American countries had led the people and their revolutionary leaders to disparage and underestimate continental co-ordination and unity within the anti-imperialist struggle. Che insists with good reason that the strategy of imperialism and native bourgeois sell-outs compels us to readjust the insurrectional strategy. He states: 'We have maintained for a long time that, given the similarities of the countries, the American struggle will eventually acquire continental dimensions.'

The continentalization of the Latin American war of liberation is a concept that the Chilean MIR has long and persistently advocated. The guerrilla struggles in Bolivia and Venezuela demonstrate that revolutionaries of the continent are prepared to consider themselves soldiers of Latin American independence. Thus do they elevate to a higher historical level the teachings implanted by the struggle for independence of the last century. . . .

The 'Letter' does not exclude Chile from this general context. Che confronts the arguments of opportunists who contend that 'the Chilean democratic tradition' makes it an exception to the pattern of hemispheric liberation struggles, which the opportunists would convert into a caricature of struggle or an 'electoral guerrilla struggle', in which even the sharks of the radical bourgeoisie might swim. Che says: 'Of course, the last country to liberate itself may well do so without armed struggle and would thus be spared the sufferings of a long and cruel war perpetrated by the imperialists. However, it might be impossible to avoid such a war and its world-wide consequences; indeed, the suffering could be worse than expected. We cannot predict the future. On the other hand, we will never succumb to the temptation to back a people who desire liberty, but who abjure the concomitant struggle in the hope of attaining liberty, as if liberty were alms to be dispensed by the victorious.'

Statement by the Political Secretariat of Chile's
Movement of the Revolutionary Left (MIR) in support
of Che Guevara's 'Message to the Tricontinental',
Estrategia (Santiago de Chile), No. 9, June 1967,
abridged.

41 The Tupamaros and the Traditional Parties of the Left
PUNTO FINAL

For reasons that have remained implicit in the past, the connections between the direct-action group and the Socialist Party have been especially strong. The development of the Tupamaro Movement and the political struggle within the Socialist Party from 1959 to the present – in its transition from the social democratic line to the Marxist–Leninist in adherence to the OLAS agreements and declarations – gradually helped to make independent the actions of those Socialist leaders and cadres who had participated from the outset in the Tupamaro group. Contributing to this autonomy was the participation of other political groupings. The Socialist Party, during the process of radicalizing its line, lacked the capacity to develop a sound organization and course of action because it was involved in an ideological struggle that required the expulsion of fractionalist tendencies seeking to control and divide the Party. To summarize, we can say that, while the splinter groups that left the Socialist Party over the last eight years have virtually disappeared from the political scene, the nucleus that generated the Tupamaro Movement has been the only one to consolidate, organize and strengthen itself. It may be said in favor of the SP that this nucleus was the only group initially inspired by the Party in accordance with a line that led, year after year, to increased radicalization and militancy. In criticism of the SP, however, the intention to maintain an organic relationship to the direct-action group was weakened by the inability of the political leaders to provide direction.

With respect to the Communist Party, the first years of Tupamaro activities seem to have been characterized by negligible or non-existent relations with it. Influential in determining this weak relationship was a certain tendency common to the work of the CP's in Latin America: any activity that they do not control is unacceptable to them. Another factor was the traditional inability of Marxist parties in Uruguay to reconcile their differences. Sendic was from the SP, and his most important connections were with the SP; thus, the CP would not assist the advancement of his movement. Finally, the most fundamental problem was that there had always existed disagreements with the CP over the aim and form of the sugar-cane workers' struggle in the first stage and over the revolutionary line and tactics of the Tupamaro Movement in its course of development and consolidation. This Movement's practical adherence to the OLAS declaration contradicts the position of the CP's of the continent concerning the road to revolution. For that reason, both Sendic and the entire movement have repeatedly been accused of 'revolutionary adventurism' by leaders and theoreticians of the CP and by its representatives in the press and media.

At the present time the National Liberation Movement (Tupamaros) exists for all; and it can be said that its work is fraternally considered by the Socialist Party, the Uruguayan Revolutionary Movement (MRO) and the Anarchist Federation of Uruguay (FAU), and that it is treated with respect by the Communist Party.

'Los tupamaros y la lucha armada', *Punto Final*
(Santiago de Chile), 2 June 1968, abridged.

e THE CONVERGENCE OF ANARCHISM ON GUEVARISM

The tradition of militant anarchism stemming from Michael Bakunin gives precedence to direct action by the workers as a condition of destroying the capitalist state. The rival tradition of Auguste Blanqui calls for an armed apparatus of professional revolutionaries for seizing political power and establishing a dictatorship of the proletariat. The Spanish anarchist in exile, Abraham Guillén, is the first to have wedded these two revolutionary traditions with Guevara's strategy of the insurrectional foco. Favoring the incorporation of a guerrilla nucleus with a mass political movement in the cities rather than the countryside, Guillén was directly influential in shaping the actions of the Tupamaros and the ERP.

42 Where, When and How to Create an Insurrectional Foco   ABRAHAM GUILLÉN

Ernesto Che Guevara is correct in that 'the insurrectional foco can create revolutionary conditions'; but, in order that David not be defeated by Goliath, it is necessary to know where, how, with how many, with what means and for what purpose the guerrillas are to direct their actions. A minority cannot attain power and fulfil its promises unless it acts in the interests of the majority, on behalf of the party of the discontented. It would be ridiculous to base a strategy on purely geographic or topographic factors alone. That would be to ignore the fact that in revolution the decisive factor is to win over the population and that the lesser factors have to do with the number of enemy forces, the terrain and armaments. . . .

In a highly urbanized civilization, a war in the mountains, when chosen as the only form of insurrectional war, is totally deficient as a rational strategy. It would lead to defeat upon defeat; for, if the cities do not enter the war or remain neutral while the guerrillas are fighting in the mountains and countryside, then the enemy force may be sufficiently resistant to prolong the war until exhaustion works to its advantage. . . .

The Spanish anarchists, who were permanent clandestine members of the Iberian Anarchist Federation (FAI), struck and disappeared. Thus they helped to win strikes, whereas the social democrats were always inclined toward arbitration with agencies of the bourgeois state. In urban guerrilla warfare for the conquest of the streets, the anarchists were the great teachers and masters, true disciples of the Blanquist tradition; but they did not take power, due to the absence of an international revolutionary program. Since it is impossible for two forces to exist in a state of permanent opposition without one eventually triumphing, the anarchists lost control of the working masses. They were incapable of defeating capitalism and establishing socialism because they had no program for taking power, for conquering the state – not even for the purpose of destroying it in order to create revolutionary power. The classic anarchists had created a myth of the state. They would have nothing to do with it, as if they were religious people who desired no contact with the devil. Consequently, they took the streets from the bourgeoisie but left that class in control of the state apparatus, which was to destroy them militarily. . . .

The theory that the revolutionary foco can create the revolutionary party – rather than the inverse – is correct. However, if the country in which the insurrection is begun has a mainly urban population, the foco will not prosper while acting alone in the mountains. It would be isolated logistically and would be unable to replace its fallen combatants with new personnel. That is what happened to Che Guevara in Bolivia in 1967. The guerrilla foco must operate in zones where the masses can be mobilized on the basis of immediate grievances, in areas distant from the control of dictatorial governments. A guerrilla force separated from the proletarian masses is isolated and will soon exhaust its initial resources. This strategic principle stands out above all the unsuccessful attempts at revolutionary war in Latin America. If the failures have been repeated, it is because this law of strategy has been ignored. It is now time to learn this law to avoid more unsuccessful insurrections.

Before starting a guerrilla war, it is necessary to create, in the city or the countryside, an essential territorial organization, an armed party, in order that the guerrillas may move back and forth between their front and the enemy's rearguard as often as required by political and strategic concerns. The guerrillas must be preceded by the territorial organization and not vice versa. The ideal situation is to have three guerrillas in the enemy rearguard for every one in the guerrilla base in the mountains.

The most vital struggle is the one that takes place amidst the populace for their control. For that purpose, juntas for national liberation must be created. These juntas will duplicate public authority in such a way that the government and its functionaries, when confronted with a parallel government, will be rendered ineffective and isolated from the general population. The old strategy had as its goal the defense of the land, inch by inch, but the new strategy has as its basic objective the control of the population.

From Abraham Guillén's introduction to the
Uruguayan edition of Che Guevara's *La guerra de
guerrillas* (Montevideo, 1968), pp. 18–22, abridged.

f THE CONVERGENCE OF PERONISM ON GUEVARISM

The three principles of Peronism – political sovereignty, economic independence and social justice – are interpreted differently by its left and right wings. Unlike the right wing, the left has consistently maintained that the Peronist program cannot be realized within a capitalist framework. During the 60s and early 70s the most outstanding representatives of the left wing included Raimundo Ongaro, head of the General Confederation of Labor of the Argentines, and Gustavo Rearte, founder of the Peronist Revolutionary Movement (MRP). Both identified the principal enemy of Argentine national liberation with US imperialism and its native supporters; furthermore, each supported the organization of guerrilla focos against the military dictatorship. Though each believed the only way to make the revolution was through appeals to Argentine nationalism, they also believed that Argentine liberation depended on a second Latin American War of Independence.

43 From Reformist Politics to Revolutionary Unity
RAIMUNDO ONGARO

Peronism was always revolutionary. Those who have not been revolutionaries are the leaders. We did not go to the Congress of Córdoba to invent a revolutionary Peronism because to do so would be to deny the historical essence of Peronism. Many leaders of the Movement were never revolutionaries and others ceased being revolutionaries when they realized that they could get rich without sacrifice.

We were at the Congress of Córdoba, and believe that it was a positive experience because we discovered an extraordinary unity there. It happened that we were all in favor of national and social liberation and that all of us finally understood that methods of struggle are going to be necessary that formerly were not even discussed.

Everyone now agrees that certain forms of struggle, such as meeting violence with violence, are going to be necessary. I have said many times: how did San Martín throw out the Spaniards? Did he do it with speeches or elections? Of course not. He did it with grenadiers; and we are the grenadiers of today. Who does not realize that today Argentina and Latin America face the Second War of Independence? If the authentic representatives of our country were here today, they would be attacking with cannons stolen from the enemy. They would not be battling within the unions. . . .

What I mean is that our country is invaded and occupied over land, air and water. Our land must be liberated. Our people in arms must do this. Naturally, since arms have been taken from the people, the people cannot do that . . . but, if each one of us had a machine-gun now, what would he do? Would we be writing and talking now? We would be taking the country, freeing the country! What we need is the machine-gun. We cannot deny the validity of the method simply because we lack the means. . . .

Peronism is the basic force the country has to produce actions for liberation. However, we should not reject the participation of Christian revolutionaries who, for various reasons, have not been active in Peronism; nor can we forget those men, especially the youth, who are militants in other cultural, labor and political groups and who have always fought for social revolution. These comrades, whose common denominator might be called the desire for socialist revolution, are also an active component in the liberation struggle.

It is our hope that these three tendencies will work together in actions so that there will arise from action and struggle a united will and purpose in order to achieve common objectives. This unity among those who wish to struggle, who never surrender, will encourage every individual to act seriously, unselfishly and courageously. There will then emerge a second stage: organic unity. In the period of organic unity, initiatives and projects will be co-ordinated and we will resolutely advance toward the taking of power.

Our most important convictions will be tested: the will to unite for struggle and the solidarity with those imprisoned, the unemployed, the persecuted and all people who dare to oppose the powerful.

The new unity we seek is what unites all of us who confront the powerful: the powerful in the Church, in the army, in the economy, in politics, in culture, and the self-styled 'ideological' and 're-volutionary' vanguards. The new unity will unite us in struggle and in action. Two men in prison together become united; that is the new unity. Two men gathered around a ballot box, planning to sabotage the election; that is the old unity. . . .

Speaking of Che Guevara, I have often said that I wished he were in Argentina so that I might have the honor of fighting by his side and with many Argentines. I would have liked to fight with him in a battle that would have meant a shorter struggle for some of the smaller countries of Latin America.

What impresses me most about Che is the contrast between his attitude and that of many political and labor leaders in our country and in other Latin American countries. It is disgusting to see how many political or labor leaders who were poor have become rich, or to see those who are still poor attempting to become wealthy. Che, in contrast, who had power and was a government minister who could have grown rich and ordered people around, fulfilled the Gospel message by shunning power and the possibility of wealth and by becoming poor and going off to fight at the side of the most impoverished and to die for them. This is a deed almost without precedent. In his calling and stewardship, he bore an astonishing resemblance to Christ.

Raimundo Ongaro, 'El peronismo fue siempre
revolucionario', *Cristianismo y Revolución* (Buenos
Aires), No. 13, 1–15 April 1969, abridged.

44 The Peronist Revolutionary Movement Outlines its Program   *MRP*

The Peronist Revolutionary Movement was established and publicly announced on 5 August 1964. That date signified the culmination of a period of maturation for an important group of authentically Peronist comrades. It was the birth of a new experience within the movement, a new style that crystallized the youthful and re-volutionary militancy, which today, with different initials and derived from diverse experiences, is building a tool for people's war, a war that will inexorably lead to national liberation and the construction of a socialist homeland. It will convert the dreams of Evita Perón into a reality; and the struggle of the people and their leader will create a world in which there will no longer exist exploiters or exploited, in which working men and women will not have to fear old age and in which the only privileged class will be the children.

After the vital experiences of the struggle in Resistencia, a necessary lesson in which we paid a great price for our errors, it was not until 18 March 1962 that we really understood the event in its true dimensions: we Peronists were unable to guarantee the splendid popular victory that we had achieved. We realized at the time that it was necessary to integrate the struggle within a single centralized political apparatus and to build a popular army capable of taking power for the people. We discarded the *coup d'état* notions which had led us to place our hope in the military, gone forever as a decent institution; and we understood that our revolutionary soldiers were revolutionaries not by profession, but because they were political militants, combatants for the cause of the people.

The maturity we had acquired enabled us to visualize the struggle on a continental level and to understand, like San Martín and Bolívar, that our destiny was linked to that of our fellow Latin Americans, who were intensifying the war of 150 years against the latest imperialism. In this second War of Independence some countries were teaching us new methods for defeating the armed forces, which had previously seemed invincible. Such was the case of heroic Cuba, which was teaching us with its example.

It was from that point of departure – the deepening of revolutionary thought in the Peronist masses, the continuing quest of their militants, the clairvoyant strategy of their leader – from that time, that the organizational objectives crystallizing on 5 August were born. The revolutionary perspective institutionalized in the historic documents of that date calls for:

—The nationalization of all basic sectors of the economy.
—Agrarian reform.
—The confiscation of monopolies.
—Worker control of production.
—Economic planning.
—Urban reform.
—The total elimination of the exploitation of man by man.
—The development of a national consciousness to serve as a basis for an authentic national mass culture.
—The defense of the rights of self-determination for all peoples and the maintenance of relations with all the peoples of the world.
—Solidarity with and support for all peoples fighting for their freedom against imperialism and colonialism. . . .

Today we would like to reaffirm some concepts that we consider fundamental, points that have led to quite a few misunderstandings with our splendid militant companions.

Peronism, as a mass movement, is a united front of classes and a national liberation movement. It is the broadest and most comprehensive political instrument for confrontation with the principal enemy: US imperialism and its indigenous lackeys.

The revolutionary period in which we live is that of national liberation; thus, it is necessary to unite all national revolutionary sectors in order to engage successfully imperialism and its agents. It is also necessary in this stage to attempt to isolate the enemy from all its natural allies. . . .

It is also incumbent upon us to encourage a policy of unity with those revolutionary sectors that we might call 'extraparty', for the purpose of developing an armed struggle to destroy the common enemy.

Finally, it is absolutely essential to develop a military-revolutionary structure that will wage the people's war, 'in which every Peronist is a combatant, be it with arms or with any other means available'. It will be the mailed fist of the people, intimately and absolutely tied to the people, which acts clandestinely in all places and which will be composed of members from all and any fronts. . . .

The qualitative change in the armed struggle, initiated by the appearance of the Peronist Armed Forces (FAP) in Taco Ralo, developed by the profoundly significant political operations of the Montoneros and exemplified by the technical prowess of the Revolutionary Armed Forces (FAR) in taking Garín, indicates to us that a new method of people's war has become institutionalized and consolidated among the militant groups. Every political analysis to be made should keep these phenomena in mind.

Statement by the Peronist Revolutionary Movement (MRP), *Cristianismo y Revolución* (Buenos Aires), April 1971, No. 28, pp. 47–9, abridged.

g CHE, CAMILO AND THE NEW CHRISTIANITY

Among the chief factors contributing to a Latin American Christianity revitalized by Guevarist precepts were Camilo Torres' decision to join the Colombian ELN and the emergence of a Camilist Movement in response to his martyrdom. The first document contains Camilo's reasons for joining the ELN: the presence in Colombia of a National Front of the principal parties of the oligarchy with legal guarantees of remaining in power – hence his call to boycott the elections – and the ELN's support of Camilo's United Front against the oligarchy. The second elucidates the basic theme of the First Camilo Torres Latin American Encounter in Montevideo: the duty of every Christian is to be a revolutionary (Camilo); the duty of every revolutionary is to make the revolution (Che). The third document relates the activities of Camilist groups in Argentina: the founding and dissemination of revolutionary religious and political journals; the mobilization of Catholic student and youth groups in Camilo Torres Commandos; the support of rank-and-file tendencies within the General Confederation of Labor; the convergence on the Peronist Movement; and the participation in armed actions with the Montoneros and Peronist Armed Forces (FAP).

45 To All Colombian Patriots! The Army of National Liberation is the Armed Embodiment of the United Front   CAMILO TORRES

Colombians:

For many years the poor people of our country have awaited the cry of battle to hurl themselves into the final struggle against the oligarchy.

On those occasions when the desperation of the people has reached its limits, the ruling class has always found a way to deceive the people, to distract them, to pacify them with formulas that always result in the same thing: suffering for the people and well-being for the priviliged class.

When the people sought a leader and found one in Jorge Eliécer Gaitán, the oligarchy murdered him. When the people asked only for peace, the oligarchy brought violence to the country. When the people could no longer stomach violence and organized the guerrillas to take power, the oligarchy invented a military coup so that the guerrillas would be deceived into surrendering. When the people called for democracy, they were again deceived by a plebiscite and a National Front which imposed upon them the dictatorship of the oligarchy.

Now the people no longer believe. The people do not believe in elections. The people know that the old legal approaches are exhausted. The people know that the only course left is armed struggle. The people are desperate and resolved to risk their lives in order that the next generation of Colombians will not be slaves. So that the children of those who are now prepared to give their lives may have an education, a roof over their heads, food, clothing and, above all, dignity. So that future generations of Colombians will have a land of their own, independent of North American power and domination.

Every sincere revolutionary has to understand that armed resistance is the only course left. The people are waiting for the leaders to issue the call to war with their presence and their examples.

I wish to tell the Colombian people that this is the moment, that I have not betrayed them. I have seen the squares of towns and cities clamoring for the unity and organization of the popular classes in order to take power. I have asked that we devote ourselves to that objective until death.

All is now ready. The oligarchy intends to arrange another electoral farce, with candidates who don't want to run but then accept the nominations, with bipartisan committees, with reform movements based on ideas and people that not only are old but have also betrayed the people. Why do we Colombians wait?

I have joined the armed struggle. In the Colombian mountains I intend to follow the war with arms in my hands until power for the people has been won. I have joined the Army of National Liberation because I found in it the same ideals as those of the United Front. I found the achievement of a mass unity based on the peasants, without differences caused by religious intolerance or antagonisms of the traditional parties. Here there is no desire to antagonize revolutionary elements of any sector, movement or party. No bossism or opportunism. The desire is to liberate the people from exploitation, the oligarchies and imperialism – not to lay down arms until power is completely in the hands of the people. The ELN accepts the platform of the United Front.

All we Colombians should mobilize for war. Day by day experienced guerrilla leaders will come forth in all corners of the country. We should be in a state of alert. We should gather together arms and munitions, seek guerrilla training, talk with our closest friends, gather clothing, provisions and drugs, be prepared for a long struggle. Let us engage the enemy in minor skirmishes, in which victories will be assured. Let us test those who call themselves revolutionaries. Let us expel the traitors. We must act unceasingly but not become impatient. In a protracted war, each will have an action to perform at some moment. What is important is that the revolution find us ready at that moment. One person will not have to do everything. We will distribute tasks. The military leaders of the United Front will build the vanguard with their acts and initiative. Let us have a firm and patient confidence in the final victory. . . .

Camilo Torres
for the Army of National Liberation (ELN)

Camilo Torres, 'Proclama de Camilo al Pueblo Desde las Montañas (January 1966), *El Camilismo en la América Latina*, edited by Enrique López Oliva (Havana, 1970), pp. 15–17, slightly abridged.

46 Bases of the Camilo Torres Latin American Encounter   JUAN GARCÍA ELORRIO

Inspired by the motto, 'The duty of every Christian is to be a revolutionary, and the duty of every revolutionary is to make revolution,' the first Camilo Torres Latin American Encounter took place in Montevideo in February 1968. There progressive Catholics from different countries of the continent discussed practical problems related to the incorporation of Christians into the developing revolutionary process.

Participating in the gathering were worker-priests, lay Catholics, militants from several leftist Catholic organizations, student and labor leaders, progressive Catholic intellectuals, delegates from several revolutionary organizations. . . .

The major report of the Encounter was given by the General Secretary of the event and leader of the Camilo Torres Commandos of Argentina, the ex-seminarian Juan García Elorrio, who stated that Camilo Torres and Ernesto Che Guevara 'are the two most exemplary representatives of the revolutionary vocation in Latin America'.

Position Paper of the Meeting in Montevideo
In view of the fact that revolution is not only permitted but required for all Christians, and that we understand it to be the most effective manner of realizing love for all mankind, we proclaim that the duty of every Christian is to be a revolutionary, and the duty of every revolutionary is to make the revolution. . . .

1 Christians must participate actively and urgently, as so many of our brothers are already doing, in the struggles of the Latin American revolution, which is now resolutely challenging US imperialism with the example and inspiration of Cuba, the first free territory of America.

2 All Christians must see that class warfare is the result of the terrible and inhuman conditions in which the worker and peasant masses live in America. Christians, transcending once and for all the wilful and self-interested misinterpretations of the Gospel, must join the class struggle on the side of those who suffer from exploitation and domination.

3 For the Latin American revolution there is only one strategy that confronts the counter-revolutionary strategy of imperialism, the OAS, the Pentagon, the gorillas and the puppet governments

subservient to Yankee strategy. Revolutionary militants must adopt the strategy of the OLAS and the revolutionary and national liberation movements, the strategy that recognizes only those revolutionary vanguards engaged in battle. It denounces the pseudo-revolutionary strategies of the Communist parties in compliance with the directives from Moscow, which advocate 'peaceful coexistence' and a sterile campaign for 'civil liberties' that are systematically trampled upon by governments. Our strategy also denounces the so-called 'Christian revolutionary' line, which has as its maximum exponent Frei and his failures and is reflected in the 'progressive' and 'developmentalist' positions of CELAM.

4 Our struggle acknowledges no frontiers and is a part of the struggles of the people of the Third World. Our revolutionary duty calls for militant solidarity with the Third World, with the millions dying of hunger and disease. In pointing out the failure of the so-called efforts to resolve the problems of the Third World and, in particular, the recent failure of the New Delhi conference, we are bringing attention to the most violent contradiction of our times: the contradiction between the wealthy and the impoverished nations, between the exploiting and the pillaged, between all forms of imperialism and suffering humanity which says 'enough!'

5 A study of the role of the Church in Latin America must conclude that the actions of John XXIII and the Vatican Council have not substantially modified the attitude of the hierarchies and the Church, which have at best realized 'progressive' advancements that are inadequate. This very limited progress does not reflect, in the eyes of the popular masses and the community, the true message that the Gospel provides at this hour in history, a message that should be translated into revolutionary action for the liberation of the whole man and all mankind.

Juan García Elorrio, 'Documento de la Jornada de
Montevideo' (June 1968), *El Camilismo en la América
Latina*, edited by Enrique López Oliva (Havana, 1970),
pp. 67–69, abridged.

47 The Role of Christians in the Revolution: In the Footsteps of Che and Camilo CASIANA AHUMADA

Comrade Casiana Ahumada, we would like to begin by asking you about Cristianismo y Revolución. *Why was it founded? For what purposes? What is it today? What is its perspective?*

In examining the various stages in the development and maturation of his Christian faith, we see that Camilo is the first to understand how the exigencies of the Gospel and those of history coincide. His death opens the possibility of a convergence of Christian practice and revolutionary action. . . .

Comrade Juan García Elorrio was one of the first youths in Buenos Aires to see in Camilo's testimony the possibility of enriching Christian faith with revolutionary experience. Juan did not personally know Camilo, but he attentively followed the priest's development: Camilo's studies as a sociologist, his quest for political action and his acceptance of armed struggle as the only valid path to revolution. Only a few months after the death of Camilo, Juan decided to spread Camilo's message with a publication that today expresses his thought and political action: the magazine *Cristianismo y Revolución*. . . .

What is the relationship of Cristianismo y Revolución *to the creation of the Camilo Torres Commandos and García Elorrio's participation in them?*

The appearance of *Cristianismo y Revolución* provoked a storm of reaction because it stated that revolutionary action was an imperative for Christians. Those reactionaries and 'progressives' who had proposed to offer a hesitant support to the Onganía government are today harshly attacked by the youthful segment of the ecclesiastical structures. These youths, having become disgusted with spiritualistic approaches, seek solidarity with those who suffer from hunger and injustice. Several groupings, including the Catholic Student Youth (JEC), the Catholic University Youth (JUC) and the Catholic universities of the interior, have approached Juan García Elorrio and agreed to develop a plan for revolutionary militancy because they feel it is their duty to participate in the transformation of a society that generates violence and exploitation. With that objective in mind, Camilo Torres Commandos are being established in Buenos Aires and in some cities of the interior. These Commandos are closely linked to the magazine that has come to be a working paper for this new tendency: revolutionary Christianity.

The assumption of that duty presupposed the realization of a series of actions designed to unmask the hierarchy and to demonstrate in practice our solidarity with the struggles of the people against the military regime.

The wisdom acquired through reflection, the experience of living with marginal sectors of society and contact with those already engaged in militant action lead us to doubt the 'Christian' character of the military and the hierarchy. The necessity of transcending the use of religious faith as a divisive factor and the need to establish a political option have led to an integration with organizations of revolutionary Peronism. García Elorrio has joined the Peronist militants. *Cristianismo y Revolución* has maintained a greater independence. Special publications have been established for political purposes: the newspaper *Che Compañero* and, later, *Con Todo*. . . .

Would you give us an idea of the revolutionary participation by the Christian movement in Argentina today? In addition, how is it related to other similar movements in the rest of Latin America?

With respect to lay Catholics, there is a growing militancy oriented principally toward Peronist organizations. On the labor scene, considerable support is given to the rank-and-file groups in the General Confederation of Labor (CGT) and in other organizations. Student support is provided by the National Union of Students (UNE). Armed action is represented by members of the Peronist Armed Forces (FAP) and the Montoneros. It is common knowledge that at least one priest, Arturo Ferre Gadea (arrested at Taco Ralo in 1967), and one deacon, Gerardo Ferrari (killed in action in 1969), belonged to FAP. The Montoneros Mario Firmenich and Carlos Ramus had been leaders of the JEC; Fernando Abal, a leader of Catholic Action (AC). These three have been identified as the principal figures in the execution of Lieutenant-General Aramburu; and the last two died while fighting against repression. Emilio Maza, Ignacio Veloz, Cristina Liprandi and a number of people on the police 'wanted' list for participation in the takeover of the Cordoban town of La Calera in July 1970 – a Montonero action – are all Peronist comrades with a pronounced adherence to Christian militancy.

Interview with Casiana Ahumada, *Pensamiento Crítico*
(Havana), No. 52, May 1971, pp. 141–4, abridged.

Part Four

*The Role of
Guevarism in the Industrially
Advanced Countries*

a URBAN GUERRILLA WARFARE

Within the developed countries the two most important urban guerrilla movements testifying to Guevarist influence were Weatherman in the US and the Red Army Fraction in West Germany. Differences in their respective strategies may be explained in part by the different milieus in which they operated: Weatherman in a country with a sizeable though dispersed Black 'internal colony' and an army of occupation in South Vietnam; the RAF in a nation where what was seen as repression of workers and students was the principal focus of opposition in the absence of internal colonialism and direct military involvement abroad. As the first document indicates, Weatherman acted as a fifth column for the Black Panthers as well as the Vietcong. In contrast, the RAF initiated military actions on the premise, first, that mass movements against repression are ineffective without armed detachments and, second, that when conditions are ripe for resisting repression it is generally too late to organize guerrillas.

48 USA: The Creation of Strategic Armed Chaos
WEATHERMAN

Because imperialism is an international system, built on worldwide domination, the strategy needed to defeat it must be an international one, attacking different peoples' common oppression by linking together their struggles for liberation.

In the imperialists' colonies, victory demands that people seize political, military, and economic control of their country from the United States. The people of Vietnam, Bolivia, Laos, etc. are engaged in nationalist wars, struggling for national self-determination, identity, and power. Militarily, their task is to defeat the occupation army, physically kicking the imperialists and their puppets out and building an independent state based on the armed power of the people.

Their struggle, nationalist in form, is of necessity internationalist as well. The Cubans won their national war by seizing power in their country, but the development of a communist society in Cuba continues to be obstructed by US imperialism in the form of blockades and embargoes, CIA counter-insurgency operations, etc., and by the continued oppression of the many remaining colonies. The ultimate success of the Cuban revolution and all revolution depends on the total worldwide destruction of imperialism and the establishment of world communism. So the Cuban people fully understand their role in creating and materially supporting the international struggle. Hence Che leaves Cuba to open another front in Bolivia. . . .

For us in the white mother country victory also means defeating the same ruling class and military machine. But the differences in our political/military situation lead us to a somewhat different strategy. We are fucked over in schools, jobs, in every social relationship, robbed of our humanity and the political power on which that must be built. We are oppressed because of class origin, as youth, as women, but not as a nation. We are a nation only in doing the shitwork and ripping off the world and accepting the privileges the rip-off produces. In white Amerika nationalism can be nothing other than a reactionary ideology, a basis for the further oppression of the world's people. Our task is not to seize state power for ourselves, but to destroy the imperialist order. What replaces it must be internationalist, with its highest priority the destruction of racism and great nation privilege and chauvinism, and restitution for Amerika's crimes through internationalization of resources, etc.

These differences in the political and military requirements for victory as between the colonies and the mother country lead not only to different military objectives and tactics, but also to qualitatively different kinds of warfare. . . .

The most striking characteristic of imperialist military organizing, its centralization, largely determines the nature of armed struggle here. The basic resources of supply, manpower, and command lie in the United States itself. Within the generally centralized octopus of power there are subordinate but essential centers. Everything has to be co-ordinated, centrally directed.

This is why the liberation struggle of the black internal colony is key. While blacks are fighting a nationalist war for self-determination, the success of their struggle depends not on kicking the imperialists out, but on destroying them completely. Black people are in a unique colonial situation because of their location in relation to the centers of power.

White revolutionaries live behind enemy lines. We are everywhere: above, below, in front, behind, and within. While we possess none of the machinery of the state, it is always close at hand. Our ability because we are white to move within the structure of the state, to locate ourselves in and around all of its institutions, opens up explosive possibilities for undermining its power. Our strategy must take into account the ways in which this particular asset can be used to provide material support for the strategy of the black colony.

Thus, the political command of means of violence, prisons, mass media, schools, election and party machinery, etc. gives the ruling class a strength which is only illusory. It is material, institutional, and rests on sand. The entire works has not been able to keep us, the youth of Amerika, from waking up and striking out at our oppression.

Our political objective is the destruction of the imperialist state, and the military conditions we face fighting within the borders of the mother country are ideal. Our strategy has to be geared toward forcing the disintegration of society, attacking at every level, from all directions, and creating strategic 'armed chaos' where there is now pig order.

National War Council of Weatherman, 'Everyone
Talks About the Weather' (December 1969), reprinted
with permission from *Weatherman*, edited by Harold
Jacobs (San Francisco, 1970), pp. 440–4, abridged.
© Copyright 1970 by Ramparts Press.

49 West Germany: When Conditions are Ripe for Armed Struggle It Will Be Too Late to Prepare for It
RED ARMY FRACTION

We affirm that the organization of armed resistance groups in West Germany and West Berlin is correct, possible and justified. We further state that it is correct, possible and justified to make urban guerrilla war here and now. . . .

We don't say that illegal armed resistance groups can take the place of legal proletarian organizations, that single actions can replace the class struggle, nor that armed struggle can replace political work on the industrial front and in the communities. We only affirm that one is necessary for the success of the other. . . .

Under the present conditions in West Germany and West Berlin we doubt the possibility of developing a unifying strategy for the working class and of creating an organization which could be the expression and initiator of the necessary unifying process. We doubt that the union of the socialist intelligentsia and the proletariat can be reached either by dogmatic explanations or by demands for unity coming from proletarian organizations. We state that without revolutionary initiative, without practical revolutionary intervention of the avant-garde, the socialist workers and the intellectuals, and without concrete anti-imperialist struggle, there will be no unifying process. . . .

The 'provisional revolutionary demands' that the proletarian organizations put up all over the place, like the struggle against the intensification of exploitation, for shorter working hours, the attacks on the waste of social wealth, attacks on productivity deals etc: these interim demands are nothing but trade union economism, as long as they don't answer the question of how to break the political, military and propaganda power of the state, which always stands in the way of these demands when they are put up in mass class struggles. If then these demands stay the same, one can only call them economistic shit – because they are not worth the revolutionary energy used up in fighting for them, and they won't lead to victory when victory means 'to accept on principle that life is not the most precious gift for a revolutionary' (Debray). With these demands trade unions can intervene – but 'the trade union politics of the working class are bourgeois working class politics' (Lenin). That's not a revolutionary method of intervention. The so-called proletarian organizations don't put forward armed struggle as an answer to the emergency laws, the Army, the Bundesgrenzschutz, the police, the Springer press. As long as they hold this position they differ from the Communist Party only by being less rooted in the masses, verbally more radical and theoretically superior. In practice they are on the same level as civil rights organizations which seek popularity at any price, and they support the lies of the bourgeoisie in implying that in this state it is still possible to straighten anything out by parliamentary means. They push the proletariat into struggles that are unwinnable in the face of the power of the state. . . .

The concept of the urban guerrilla comes from Latin America. Here, the role of the urban guerrilla can only be the method of revolutionary intervention of generally weak revolutionary forces.

Urban guerrilla warfare is based on the analysis that . . . when the conditions are right for armed struggle it will be too late to prepare for it. Even when the conditions for revolutionary struggle are better than they are now, there will be no revolutionary orientation without revolutionary initiative in a country with the potential state power, and broken and weak revolutionary traditions, of the West German Republic.

Urban guerrilla war is the consequence of the negation of parliamentary democracy by the elected representatives themselves;

it is the inevitable answer to the emergency laws, and the laws which gave hand grenades to the police in Berlin. It is the preparedness to struggle with the very means that the system appropriates for itself to eliminate its enemies. . . . It can blunt the weapons of the system, viz., the illegalization of communists, by organizing an underground which is not easy prey for the police. . . .

Urban guerrilla war aims to destroy the domination of the state by striking at single weak points, and to destroy the myth of the omnipotence of the state and its invulnerability.

Urban guerrilla war demands the organization of an illegal apparatus which includes weapons, cars, flats and documents. What one needs to know in particular about this, Marighela describes in his *Mini-manual of the Urban Guerrilla*. . . .

Our original concept of organization implied the relation of urban guerrilla war to work at the base. We imagined that each of us could simultaneously work in communities or in factories with existing social groups, and so influence discussions and gather new experiences. This has turned out to be impossible, because the control which the political police has over these groups, their meetings, dates, the content of their discussions, is so far developed that one can't work with them if one wants to be free from police control.

'The Concept of the Urban Guerrilla', *Armed Resistance in West Germany: Documents of the Red Army Fraction* (Stoke Newington, 1972), pp. 36–7, 42–7, abridged.

b EXTRAPARLIAMENTARY MASS OPPOSITION

The principal alternative to urban guerrilla warfare in the advanced countries is the Guevarist strategy of creating continuing chaos in production. In balance this strategy has been more effective than that of either Weatherman or the RAF. *In Italy* Lotta Continua *thrives on techniques of industrial paralysis and sabotage, which compare favorably to those of the Peronist Revolutionary Movement in Argentina that contributed to the ousting of the military dictatorship.*

50 Italy: Strategic Chaos in Production is a Political Objective of the Workers *LOTTA CONTINUA*

What makes the proletarian struggle revolutionary? Is it the capacity of damaging, to the point of undermining, the economic roots of capitalist economic development, or is it the consciousness stimulated in the masses of the necessity for overthrowing capitalist power and establishing communism? Put in these terms the alternative is mistaken. To isolate a presumed objective fact – the economic damage inflicted by the struggle – and a presumed subjective fact – the growth of communist consciousness – is possible only by ignoring the reality of class struggle. . . .

When we say that the crisis is a specific goal of the proletarian struggle, we have no intention of separating . . . the economic crisis from the political one. The crisis into which Italian capitalism is sinking is not a temporary productive crisis, but the progressive destruction by its own hands of all those conditions which bind the proletariat to exploitation and subordination. The economic discipline imposed by the laws of productivity is inseparable from the political discipline of the laws of the state.

Narrow trade unionism, in this perspective, lends a hand to the opportunism of those who confuse revolution with a putsch.

It is a calumny hurled by the owners and trade-union revisionists against the class struggle when they explain the conflict at FIAT in these terms: 'A few hoodlums exploiting the rigidity of the productive cycle can block production.' A calumny with short legs: it would be enough to get rid of those few hoodlums and perhaps appeal to the mass of judicious workers to end the mischief. In fact those 'hoodlums' are not one-sided at all; they are not worried about production or consciousness in isolation. Their daily experience has made them dialectical.

This is why they do not hesitate to block production, and to block it in the surest way: through direct action by the great majority of the workers. Two complementary news items give a clear idea of what type of crisis the owners have to face: 'Today we were ten thousand demonstrating,' and 'Today not one car has been produced.' These are the facts of workers' action. Let simple trade unionists and 'conscience-raisers' make their best of them.

What, then, at this point of the revolutionary process, is workers' autonomy? What are its determining characteristics? In the first place, it is the explicit and radical refusal of wage-labor and of the laws that govern it. The workers' estrangement from work becomes a conscious and programmatic affirmation: to damage production, to abolish the material incentives intended to make the workers responsive to increments in productivity, to refuse economic and normative divisions, to reject the pace of work, unhealthy environmental conditions, work schedules and work shifts, etc. These ideas are already present in every factory. But in the more advanced struggles they are openly asserted in the name of the crisis of power: production is a concern of the owners; the crisis of production is a political aim of the workers. . . .

The second distinctive characteristic of workers' autonomy, strictly tied to the first, is the unmasking of the counter-revolutionary role of the trade unions and of the parliamentary parties, and the explicit anticontractual organization of the struggle.

The trade union is the essential instrument for imprisoning the class struggle within the rules of capitalist economic development. The parliamentary parties, which call themselves workers' parties, are the essential instrument for returning the struggle to the democratic bourgeois game for the conservation of the system. And it is not a coincidence that, in view of the extent of the workers' struggle, this fundamental distinction has emerged with more clarity than ever: on one side, those who, like the Italian Communist Party (PCI), appropriate for themselves the responsibility for productive development; on the opposite side, those who, like the workers' autonomous vanguard, act to generalize and make permanent and irremediable the productive crisis of capital. . . .

In substance the problem is only one. The bourgeoisie will undergo an economic-social crisis of great magnitude and will seek to emerge from it without transferring the class conflict to an openly military terrain, after having inflicted on the workers' offensive a defeat of historical proportions.

To obtain this it will have to opt for a tough government prepared to repress with harshness public manifestations of the struggle – particularly in the south – and to outlaw 'extraparliamentary' activities, to give its seal of approval to massive punitive firings against any expression of autonomous workers' protests. If the weight of this repression . . . prevails, then the workers' struggle will not suffer a provisional halt but will be thrown years back, and a new equilibrium based on a more rigid authoritarianism and on a long economic stagnation will emerge. If, on the contrary, the offensive capacity of the working class is able to resist the attack against its vanguards and link itself to the more general proletarian revolt caused by the worsening conditions of the masses, capitalism will have no more cards to play than those of a military regime directly sustained by US imperialism.

It will have nothing left to do but to seek refuge in the hands of fascist and protofascist forces, which have continued to vegetate as an inelegant but necessary reserve on the periphery of the 'democratic' bourgeois development.

At that point the bourgeoisie will open the extreme phase of class struggle, that of the armed revolutionary struggle. Becoming aware of the inevitability of this process, of the shallowness of every other alternative, is necessary for all of us. For two decisive reasons.

First, without this awareness we will never be able to readjust our tasks, our way of thinking. It is a sign of the influence of the bourgeoisie on every one of us: underestimating, willingly or not, the problem of revolutionary illegality. Second, we must transform our style of work and our organization, in such a way that we will know how to face any modification imposed on the conditions of our actions.

In immediate terms this means that the next steps of our activity may face obstacles we have not yet known: from being declared outlaws to being impeded in the diffusion of propaganda, materials, etc. It is possible to face these problems only by making completely responsive all the comrades, above all the workers. In general, the organizational leap we must make should assure the maximum of centralization with the maximum of initiative.

'Situazione politica generale e nostri compiti',
Comunismo (Milan), No. 1, Fall 1970, pp. 42–4, 56–7,
abridged. From the proceedings of the National
Convention of Lotta Continua in Turin, 25–26 July
1970.

Bibliographical note

As yet there is no complete edition of Guevara's works. The most exhaustive is the Cuban edition published by Casa de las Américas, *Obras 1957–1967*, 2 vols. (Havana, 1970). This collection contains two crucial essays and a major policy address not included in John Gerassi's *Venceremos! The Speeches and Writings of Ernesto Che Guevara* (New York and London, 1968), still the most complete, if occasionally inaccurate, English edition of Che's writings. An English translation of his essay 'Tactics and Strategy of the Latin American Revolution' can be found in Rolando E. Bonachea and Nelson P. Valdés, *Che: Selected Works of Ernesto Guevara* (Cambridge, Mass., and London, 1969), and of his article 'Banking, Credit and Socialism' in Bertram Silverman, *Man and Socialism in Cuba: The Great Debate* (New York, 1971). Che's policy address, 'La influencia de la Revolución Cubana en la América Latina' (May 1962), remains untranslated.

The first comprehensive and detailed account of Guevara's intellectual and institutional legacy is in Donald C. Hodges, *The Latin American Revolution* (New York, 1974). A fascinating historical review of the principal rural guerrilla movements in Latin America is provided by Richard Gott, *Guerrilla Movements in Latin America* (London, 1970; New York, 1971), of which the urban counterpart is by James Kohl and John Litt, *Urban Guerrilla Warfare in Latin America* (Cambridge, Mass., 1974). The single most influential work on urban guerrilla warfare is *Estrategia de la guerrilla urbana* (Montevideo, 1966) by Abraham Guillén, whose lessons drawn from the Uruguayan and Brazilian urban guerrillas are available in Hodges, *Philosophy of the*

Urban Guerrilla: The Revolutionary Writings of Abraham Guillén (New York, 1973).

Among useful companion volumes to the present selection are those by Gerassi, *The Coming of the New International* (New York, 1971), and by Hodges and Shanab, *National Liberation Fronts 1960/1970* (New York, 1972), each containing a broad assortment of documents from Latin America. Unabridged versions of the most important revolutionary tracts inspired by Guevarism can be found in Vania Bambirra, *Diez años de insurrección en américa latina*, 2 vols. (Santiago de Chile, 1971), and in the anonymously edited *América latina en armas* (Buenos Aires, 1971).

Of the few bibliographies covering the impact of Guevarism and the Cuban Revolution on insurrectionary movements in Latin America, the most detailed are those included in the works by Hodges and Gott, and in an unpublished dissertation by David A. Crain, *The Course of the Cuban Heresy: The Rise and Decline of Castroism's Challenge to the Soviet Line in the Latin American Marxist Revolutionary Movement, 1963–1970* (Indiana University, Bloomington, 1971).

Many of the documents, articles and speeches in the text are available in the English editions of *Tricontinental* (Havana) and of the weekly *Granma* (Havana), the official review of the Communist Party of Cuba. The North American Congress on Latin America publishes a monthly review, *NACLA's Latin America & Empire Report* (NACLA East: P.O. Box 57, Cathedral Station, New York, N.Y. 10025; NACLA West: Box 226, Berkeley, Calif. 94701), which also occasionally reproduces documents by guerrilla movements. Also important, but available only in Spanish, are the documents by guerrilla movements reproduced in *Marcha* (Montevideo), *Cristianismo y Revolución* (Buenos Aires), *Pensamiento Crítico* (Havana) and *Punto Final* (Santiago de Chile). These periodicals are available in the special Latin American collection of the Library of the University of Florida in Gainesville.

Among the accessible English editions of the works of Fidel Castro are those by Rolando E. Bonachea and Nelson P. Valdés, *Fidel Castro: Revolutionary Struggle 1947–58* (Cambridge, Mass., and London,

1972), and Martin Kenner and James Petras, *Fidel Castro Speaks* (New York and London, 1969), covering the later period from 1959 to 1968. Régis Debray's early essays, 'Castroism: The Long March in Latin America' and 'Problems of Revolutionary Strategy in Latin America', are available in Robin Blackburn's *Strategy for Revolution: Essays on Latin America by Régis Debray* (New York and London, 1970).

213